THE DIVINE PRAYER

God of life, God of horn,
I praise thee for the peaceful dawn.
All Nature from creation hewn
Restores my spirit in the noon.
Goddess fair, Goddess kind,
With evening's close, my troubles bind.
Blessed be!

CONTENTS

Chapter 9

GRIMOIRE OF ENCHANTMENT MAGICK 156

WHAT IS SORCERY?

n this book you will find complete instruction on real, practical sorcery — magick at your fingertips, so to speak. It will tell you what sorcery really is, what it isn't, and how it all came about. You'll find out how all the different kinds of magick really work, how to choose the right magick to get the job done, how to protect yourself and work safely, and how to use your latent psychic ability to strengthen your magick. You'll learn about magickal tools and equipment, and about performing rituals and casting strong spells. You'll also get full instructions, a list of equipment, and details of the preparations needed should you want to take the Highest Initiation into the Craft of Sorcery. In short, beginners will have no problem in using this book to get started, and the experienced will have no problem finding new material and ideas.

This book is for anyone who wants to understand or develop the art of sorcery. It's a no-nonsense book with no waffle or make-believe; everything in these pages is both possible and proven by sorcery already. It's more than just a textbook on sorcery, and more than just a book on magick, witchcraft, paganism, shamanism, and spiritual growth. Everyone can use this book to some degree: from the complete beginner to the age-honored mage who already works way beyond natural forces.

Perhaps you've never tried your hand at real magick (the "k" on the end is there only to distinguish it from "stage magic," make-believe, and parlor tricks). Perhaps you just have a sense that there's more to you than the reflection you see in the mirror. Perhaps you just want to know if it's really real. Or maybe you're a witch looking for more strings to your bow, as they say.

Whatever the case, if you want to progress in magickal works and find your full potential, this is a good place to start. Let's begin by taking a look at magick's practitioners and their similarities and differences — after all, that's what you're going to be...

SORCERER, WITCH, AND SHAMAN

Someone who practices magick might be described as a witch, a wizard, a warlock, a mage, a sorcerer, a shaman, a magic-user, a cleric, a druid, a dream-weaver, a soothsayer, a fortune-teller, a healer, a seer, a wise man or wise woman, a crone, a hag, an ambassador, or any other self-appointed title. The three most used general titles are without doubt the sorcerer, the witch, and the shaman.

First definition: Sorcerer (optionally Sorceress):
"a person [of either sex] who uses magic power or ability"

Second definition: Witch (optionally Wizard):
"a person [of either sex] who uses magic power or ability"

Third definition: Shaman:
"a person [of either sex] who uses magic power or ability"

Those definitions may well be correct in isolation, but they're not a lot of use in sorting out the real meanings of the titles. The reason is simple: They're all true but missing some subtle detail about which branches of magick they tend to be associated with.

First, the Sorcerer...

When you hear the word "sorcerer," do you by any chance think of a wizard such as the great Merlin of the King Arthur legends? A tall, gray-haired, long-bearded man, perhaps many centuries old, who boldly wields power, knowledge, and wisdom that has been kept back from ordinary men by the gods themselves? He would probably make a good chess player too, for all his cunning and artifice. Well, that image isn't strictly correct, either.

The sorcerer (or sorceress, if you wish) is somebody who uses magick that operates beyond the normal accepted laws of nature and physics. True sorcerers are those who are able to alter physical appearances, composition, energies, or forces. They can cause changes in the physical world by their magick and can cause unusual phenomena in the spiritual world, even bridging the otherwise difficult transition between the physical and spiritual environments. Sorcerers are perhaps more like the Hollywood image of wizards than are witches or shamans, but not necessarily so dramatic. Sorcerers are able to change an event or a situation — rather than using the witch technique of affecting the way in which the event comes about.

Second, the Witch...

Now there's a title that conjures up one of two basically false images. When you hear the word "witch," you might think of a hunchbacked old woman with wrinkles that put prunes to shame and warts that make frogs jealous, dressed in a tatty black cape. Perhaps she has a black cat named Pyewacket or maybe Mephistopheles? The other image that may spring to mind is the more modern, updated Hollywood variety, which tends to be a beautiful young woman, say late twenties to early thirties, with alluring attire, long, straight hair, and a pale white face.

What is a witch then? Well, the word gets all tied up with that other misunderstood term, paganism. To be pagan simply means to be "outside of the Hebraic church" — meaning not a Jew, a Christian, or a Muslim. Almost all branches of religion based on those three sets of beliefs frown on the idea of using magick. That's because they are all based on the idea of an all-powerful God who assumes responsibility for the day-to-day running of creation, which leaves us mere mortals with no reason to use magick. Therefore, anyone who practices magick in any way, shape, or form must also be interfering with that all-powerful God's work. In fact, to use magick must be, in that view, to run against the ultimate will of God. That makes any magickal practitioner a heretic and therefore fit to be cast out of the church organization. That makes all magick users pagan, whether they like it or not, and whether they know it or not. This, of course, means that there are literally hundreds of branches of paganism, but don't let that confuse you. The whole point is that in paganism you don't need to conform to somebody else's views.

So witches in the most basic form are pagans who use magick of some sort. But that applies to all the other titles too. The difference is in what witches do with magick, and which kinds of magick they employ. Witches generally use magick that operates within the accepted laws of nature and physics, preferring to change the way an event is brought about rather than to directly alter the event itself.

While a sorcerer might use a growth ritual to improve the year's harvest of grain, a witch would most likely use a growth potion made from herbs and plant extracts. And where a sorcerer may choose to cure an illness using a spell or a charm, a witch might choose to use more "natural" remedies — a poultice, herb tea, lotions, and the like.

So witches may be thought of as "natural magick users," often using nature directly instead of what Hollywood would call "magic." Witches tend to develop a keen knowledge of nature, plants, herbs, seasons, times, moon cycles, human and animal characteristics, psychology, and so forth. True natural witches will be able to tell you when your cat is unwell simply by observing the cat rather than by any magick or divination. Witches maintain close links with Mother Nature — their Mother Earth. They care about the environment and they care for people and animals, even plant life.

There's much more to know about paganism so we'll take a more detailed look at it all a little later on in this chapter.

In the meantime, it will help to have a little background on Gardnerian Wicca (the branch of witchcraft named after Gerald Gardner). It seems to be the dominant witch tradition worldwide at this time, although it has been subject to a lot of criticism and reinterpretation from all quarters. It is centered on the worship of the Goddess and her consort, the Horned God, who are represented in a coven by the High Priestess and High Priest. As you'd expect, nature is honored, as is the acceptance of all living things. The belief in reincarnation is emphasized, and the Wiccan Rede (code of ethics) of harming no living thing is followed strictly. Gardnerian witches normally observe all eight pagan "Sabbats" (the main pagan festivals of the year). Initiation into a Gardnerian coven is usually given by the High Priestess or High Priest, and initiates enter the Craft in "perfect love and perfect trust," meaning that they must trust their fellow coveners. Men are initiated into the coven by the High Priestess, and women are initiated by the High Priest. In general, the coven hierarchy has three degrees of advancement, traditionally separated by at least a year and a day. Only a third-degree witch may become a High Priestess or High Priest, and the High Priestess is always considered the head of the coven. Rituals are performed within a magick circle and, while many covens still prefer traditional "skyclad" (nude) worship, many now worship wearing robes.

And finally, the Shaman...

The shaman is often mistakenly seen as a drum-bashing, partly clad jungle native with a bone through his nose, a shark-tooth necklace, and a strong desire to burn the white hunter after removing his heart by hand. I'm sure I don't need to tell you how wrong that is, do I?

Shamans are even more in tune with nature than the witches we've already talked about. They communicate with inner spiritual planes and other worlds through trances (altered states of consciousness) often achieved naturally through meditation or through other techniques. They strive to stay in tune with everything that nature offers, from which they extract every scrap of wisdom and teaching. Good examples of shamans are the classic Native American trackers or mountain hunters who have a seemingly astonishing eye, nose, ear, and taste for detail.

It's important to realize that you can't easily separate the witch from the shaman, or indeed from the sorcerer, as they all use parts of each other's skill-sets. There are areas of crossover between all these categories of magick user — sometimes small areas, sometimes huge. A true shaman would ideally never learn anything by inheritance. In other words, they don't learn what they hear from other people; they learn what they see, hear, smell, touch, and even taste in nature itself.

A most appropriate story...

There was once a village that was unfortunate enough to have its own witch, its own sorcerer, and its own shaman. The three magick users would mostly keep themselves to themselves and their paths seldom crossed.

One day, a large brown bear got into a fight with a puma in the woods — a dispute over their hunting territories near the village. The puma injured the bear so severely that, as the giant bear stumbled onto the only road leading into the village, he dropped down dead. The villagers heard the noise and came running to see what had happened. They tried to move the bear from the road and failed. Nobody was willing to cut the bear up. Nobody wanted to burn the bear in case the forest caught fire. They couldn't move him — he was just too big.

The whole village came to a standstill as all the people flocked out to see the bear's body that was blocking the whole road. Within the hour, the village elder summoned his council of advisors to his chambers and asked them for their advice. One suggested calling the witch. Another suggested the services of the shaman. Yet another suggested summoning the sorcerer. One suggested a crane but sadly, being eight hundred years too early, was dismissed on grounds of lunacy. Anyway, the three magick users were called upon to dispose of the huge bear's body quickly and safely.

As they stood at the side of the blocked road, the villagers watched with anticipation to see who would solve the problem. First, the witch stepped up to the body and dabbed an herbal lotion on its head. She cast a couple of spells and proclaimed that the herbal mixture would decompose the body very rapidly. Alas, it made no significant progress. The witch and her supporters went home disappointed.

Next, the sorcerer stepped forward and waved his hands in the air above the body, commanding it to rise into the air and cast itself aside. The body quivered slightly and then dropped heavily to the ground in just as awkward a position. The sorcerer and his followers headed back home disappointed.

Finally it was the shaman's turn. He turned to the villagers around him and told them to follow him home. With the people at a safe distance, a small group of big cats slinked out of the trees and devoured the corpse in a few short minutes.

The moral of the story: It doesn't matter what you are or who you are. What really matters is what you do and why. Witches, shamans, and sorcerers are all equally valuable, but sometimes a different method or motive may be called for to complete the job. Be who you want to be.

MISUNDERSTOOD MAGICK

The trouble with magick is that it tends to be badly misunderstood. A lot of myths, legends, stories, plays, and films revolve around witches, wizards, magicians, sorcerers, and gods. Not surprisingly, the writers of these stories have used a certain amount of inventiveness in deciding how magick is used and what it can do. For this reason, there are many stereotypes of witches and wizards, and even of magick rituals! Some are based on truth, while others are nothing more than fantasy.

Far, far away in the dawn of a distant land of mist and mountains, a man enrobed in white silk sits quietly alone on a grassy peak. To his left is a narrow clearing in front of an opening in the mountain rock, inside which the embers of an hours-old fire still glow. To his right, morning dew has formed delicately over the fragrant moss, flowers, and wild grass that adorn the rocky slope that descends into the mist of the deep valley. He opens his dark, peaceful eyes, beholds the wondrous sight that surrounds him, and utters a small incantation before gently rising to rekindle the fire from the night before. This man knows nature intimately, and nature knows his face from every bright new morning on this mountainside. This is the Wise Man of Tibet, right?

No, it isn't — it's just silly. Well, it's highly unlikely, anyway. The point is that before you begin to look at real magick in the real world, you'll need to forget everything you think you already know from all those stories and films.

Maybe you're thinking that magick can do this or that. Well, maybe it can and maybe it can't — the fact is that you can't depend on what you've heard from a playwright. All you need to do is make sure that you know who you are and what you're willing to do. That determines whether you're a sorcerer, a witch, or anything else.

MAGICK'S HISTORY

Before you can see where something will take you in the future, it's a good idea to understand the past. History allows us to learn from the mistakes and successes of those who came before us. The history of magick is a long and complicated subject, with contributions from literally every country, tribe, and tongue. Fortunately, there are a few key facts that can help us understand the directions magick has taken over the years and, most important, how those directions came to be.

Long before the Hebrew Books of Law (the Torah) were written, and before their stories took place, there was something we now call the Old Religion. It formed the beginnings of a human appreciation of the Creator, and developed rapidly through the ages in every political, social, and geographical situation. The ancient Egyptians had their array of gods and goddesses in the form of humans, animals, and spirits. Each one represented a particular aspect of the Goddess or the God. The ancient Greeks developed a belief system, and they in turn had their own gods and goddesses. The Roman Empire had its own pantheon of gods and goddesses, most of whom corresponded in character and function to their Greek counterparts.

All over the world, thousands of small pockets of Old Religion belief have surfaced over the years. Sadly, many have disappeared.

One thing remains certain: What we call paganism today predates the Judaic and Islamic religions, and is the same thing as the Old Religion, which ancient (pre-Judaic) people knew as their way of life.

This is the origin of magick as we know it today — the way of the pagan, the way of the witch, the way of the druid, the way of the shaman, the way of the sorcerer. In order to understand where our modern view of magick and spiritual development comes from, we need to see how it came about, and how it has been influenced over the ages.

One major disaster threatened to suppress paganism and the use of magick for all time — "the witch trials," or perhaps more appropriately, "the burning times."

It was in 1320 that the Catholic Inquisition added witchcraft to its list of heresies in order to combat the growing interest in paganism that was eroding the Christian Church — and consequently its finances! The infamous Inquisition was made up of zealous volunteers who wanted to eliminate "heretics" — those who believed anything other than accepted Christian doctrine. From their origins in Rome and Spain, inquisitors were soon to be found in every country across Europe and, with the global spread of Christianity in the following three centuries, they were eventually present in most of the known world.

Many styles of torture had been devised to inflict excruciating pain on victims without actually killing them, and the worst of these were turned upon those accused of witchcraft, particularly in Germany, France, and Spain, where thousands of people suffered at the hands of the Inquisition. The inquisitors followed procedures set forth by the Dominican monks of Pope Innocent VIII, who issued a papal bull against witches in 1484. First, the accused were told that they must confess their heresies. Regardless of confession or denial, they were stripped, shaved, pricked with needles, and finally examined for "marks of the devil" (pity those who had birthmarks!). The tortures visited upon them were many and varied: In France the rack was favored. In other countries, sharp prongs and hot metal were the approved technique. Every sensitive part of the body was a potential target — in particular the fingernails, palms, wrists, teeth, eyes, and feet. There was seemingly no end to the inventiveness of the inquisitor!

Even when tortured, many refused to admit to things that simply weren't true; they were accused of being aided by the devil. As the interrogation proceeded, a clerk would write down all that was said — and a few things that weren't said! To add insult to injury (quite literally), the inquisitors and their aides were paid out of seized funds belonging to their prisoners. If the accused were too poor, their families would be made to pay instead.

One of the earliest European mass witch-hunts took place in Arras, France, from 1459 to 1460. Most of the accused were burned at the stake during that time. The problem began at Langres in 1459 when a hermit, who was arrested for heresy, admitted to attending a pagan Sabbat, naming a prostitute and an elderly poet of Arras as his companions. He and his companions were quickly interrogated, tortured, and finally burned at the stake. A widening pool of accusations, arrests, tortures, and confessions spread like wildfire through the whole region — people of all ages and classes were arrested. The inquisitor was spurred on by two fanatical Dominican monks who believed that a third of Europe was involved in witchcraft. Anyone who protested against the burning of an accused witch was, in their opinion, also a witch. Generally, prisoners would confess to whatever the inquisitors suggested. They also named other innocent people in accordance with the inquisitors' leading questions. The inquisitors would promise them their freedom in return for confessions or accusations, but they were sentenced to death anyway.

Soon enough, the Arras witch-hunt took a heavy toll on business in that previously thriving manufacturing and trade center. To be associated with anyone in Arras was just too dangerous! At the close of the year 1460 the Duke of Burgundy called a halt to the Inquisition, and in 1461 the parliament of Paris demanded the release of all surviving prisoners. It took another thirty years before the parliament condemned such cruelties in France.

Of course, Arras was just one of thousands of mass witch-hunts across Europe. During the 16th and 17th centuries more than 100,000 people in Germany were tortured and murdered as a result of being accused of witchcraft. The witch-hunts were normally led by fanatical rulers who were being encouraged behind the scenes by the Church. Some of the worst persecutions took place in Bamberg, a small state ruled by Gottfried Johann George II Fuchs von Dornheim. Many rich and powerful people stood accused, their property and assets confiscated by the inquisitors. As a result, Dornheim became a very wealthy man, and, in 1627, he built a witch prison that contained specially constructed "interrogation" chambers. After years of outcry from the people of Bamberg, in 1630 and 1631 Emperor Ferdinand issued mandates opposing the persecutions. Just one year later, in 1632, Dornheim died, and his tyrannical rule of Bamberg ended.

Towards the end of the 17th century, the Church began to lose its absolute political and legal authority, and the European Inquisition started to collapse at last.

Perhaps even more famous was the witch hysteria that erupted in Salem, Massachusetts, at the end of the 17th century and lasted for many years. The prison that housed the accused was a filthy, rat-infested dungeon, measuring some 70 by 280 feet (21 × 84m). There were no bars, as the strangely stoical prisoners simply obeyed instructions and accepted their punishment. Once again, prisoners were made to pay for their keep and were left short of water to increase their desire to confess.

Perhaps the strangest thing about Salem's new prison was that, despite its terrible conditions, it turned into a social gathering place. The prison staff would sell alcohol to people who came in at night to play chess. For a bail bond of one pound, prisoners could obtain a day release to visit their families — but they had to return at night. And, in general, they did!

Not surprisingly, many of the victims died in the prison, at which point the family had to pay to have the body removed and disposed of. As with the previous European witch trials, the salaries of the magistrate, sheriff, hangman, and other staff were paid by the accused, or their families. The prisoners were also charged for their chains, their cuffs, and even the time taken for their interrogation. Those who had plenty of money (a rarity among Puritans) were sometimes able to bribe their way out of prison altogether. Those that weren't so fortunate would be taken from the prison by oxcart to the gallows hill where their bodies were left hanging, plainly visible from the center of town. Eventually, with the end of the Salem witch hysteria, the prison was closed. In point of fact, the prison has been largely restored and has been open to the public as a historical museum since 1935.

With this checkered history in mind, it may not be surprising that paganism is still a very much misunderstood subject. In the pages to come, you'll find out what paganism is all about and, perhaps more important, what it isn't about. All forms of paganism have been misrepresented over the ages; history has already shown us how disastrous the consequences of ordinary fear and hysteria can be. On the bright side, though, we can learn from the past and begin to help those around us to understand this fast-growing system of faith and spirituality.

WHAT IS PAGANISM?

Paganism is a practical and spiritual way of life that has its roots in the ancient nature religions of the world. As we've seen, it is principally rooted in the Old Religion of Europe and Africa, though many pagans today also find great worth in the indigenous beliefs of other countries. Pagans celebrate the sanctity of nature, acknowledging the Divine in everything. The Divine, as seen in nature, is that immense and unknowable power that makes up and supports the fabric of everything in creation, both seen and unseen. Such belief in the sacredness of all things can be found worldwide. This is the pagan heritage, which interprets many of the beliefs and values of our ancestors in forms adapted to modern life. What is important is not necessarily the historical validity or political attainability of such visions, but the direction in which those inspirations channel our energy, our potential, and our creativity.

Pagans honor the Divine in all its aspects, whether male or female, as parts of the sacred whole. Every man, woman, and child is, to a pagan, a beautiful and unique being. The woods and open spaces of the land, home to wild animals and birds, are cherished. Paganism stresses personal spiritual experience, and pagans often find this experience through their relationship with the natural world. They seek spiritual union with Divinity by attuning to the tides of nature and by exploring their inner selves, as reflected in others. Pagans believe that they should meet the Divine, in whatever form they perceive it, face-to-face and within their own experience rather than through an intermediary. Although some paths do have leaders and teachers, these people act as facilitators, using their wisdom and experience to help guide those in their care toward discovering their own sense and interpretation of the Divine. Pagan rites and traditions help us harmonize with the natural cycles of ourselves and of our world, so they are often held at the turning points of the seasons, at the major phases of the moon and sun, and at times of transition in life.

There are a great variety of hues within the broad spectrum of paganism. This reflects the vast range of spiritual experience, for it is believed that

everyone is unique and so everyone's spirituality must be equally unique. Some pagans follow multiple gods and goddesses, their names familiar from the pages of folklore and mythology; others focus on a single life force of no specific gender; still others devote themselves to a cosmic couple — Goddess and God, or Lord and Lady. Pagans celebrate their diversity because they believe that each person should find his or her spirituality according to the dictates of the quiet, inner voice of the soul. For this reason, they respect all sincere religions, and do not proselytize or seek converts.

In these days of eco-awareness, pagans are often at the forefront of environmental movements and thought. Pagans of all paths respect the rights of every living soul, whether human, animal, plant, or rock. They are mindful of the action of cause and effect, whether by thought or deed, upon the creatures of the Earth. All pagans must accept responsibility for themselves, both spiritually and in the things they do. Paganism encourages free thought, creative imagination, and practical human resourcefulness, holding that these are fundamental to living in harmony with the rhythms of the natural world.

In summary, then:

❖ Paganism is both a spiritual and a practical way of life.

❖ Paganism is the Old Religion (before Judaism, Islam, and Christianity).

❖ Paganism is not a religion of the book and seeks no converts.

❖ Pagans worship God as the Creator.

❖ Pagans celebrate nature and the Divine in all Creation.

❖ Pagans seek unity with God through nature and spirituality.

❖ Pagans are often at the forefront of environmental care movements.

❖ Pagans accept all sincere religions as equally valid.

MISCONCEPTIONS ABOUT PAGANISM

Perhaps because paganism encompasses so many different groups of people and belief systems — all at the same time — hundreds of misconceptions surround it. In most cases, the word "pagan" evokes the image of a tall, grim figure practicing evil magic in a darkened cave, or perhaps a ring of people dancing around in a forest clearing at night, clad in nothing but "devils' horns."

What my dictionary says...
pagan (**peí-gan**) *n.* 1. a person who is not a Christian, Jew, or Muslim. 2. a

person who is without any religion; heathen. ~*adj.* 3. of pagans. 4. irreligious. [Church Latin *paganus civilian* (hence, not a soldier of Christ)]— paganism *n.*

heathen (**heé-then**) *n.*, pl. -thens or then. 1. a person who does not acknowledge the God of Christianity, Judaism, or Islam; pagan. ~*adj.* 2. of or relating to heathen peoples. [Old English]

Common misconception: "Pagans worship Satan."

Not true. In fact, most pagans don't acknowledge the existence of Satan (which is the Christian, Jewish, and Islamic personification of evil itself) — in exactly the same way they don't acknowledge the single literal Christian, Jewish, and Islamic paternal God figure. You can't worship something that you don't acknowledge. Due to the huge number of popularized horror and sci-fi genre movies from the 1970s onwards, Satanism has become entangled in the common perception of paganism. Satanists aren't pagans — they're really Christian heretics, adopting the Christian belief system but choosing to oppose God instead of siding with Him. You'd probably be surprised at how many of the people you know are technically pagan in their beliefs and ways of life.

Common misconception: "Pagans don't believe in God."

Not true. Paganism does not accept the single patriarchal figure of God as defined by Judaism, Christianity, and Islam. Pagans do believe in God, the Creator, but within that overall God there is a male persona (the God) and a female persona (the Goddess) who are equal in every way. Each of these may then be split into many more "gods" and "goddesses" from various myths and legends, personifying more specific characteristics of the God or the Goddess, and providing simpler ways of comprehending the many facets of the larger overall God. Because of the wide variety of pagan traditions and cultures worldwide, the God and the Goddess have become known by many names, but they all refer to the same overall God in whom pagans believe. Most pagans will agree that Jews, Christians, and Muslims are worshipping this same overall God, but that they are sadly missing the whole female persona.

Common misconception: "Pagans hold ritual sacrifices."

Not true. That would be the old horror-movie typecast Satanist. Even

modern-day Satanists don't all indulge in such practices! The gods of paganism don't demand sacrifices.

Common misconception: "Pagans are all witches."

Not necessarily true, though some pagans may call themselves witches, wizards, or warlocks. All branches of paganism are aimed at the development of an individual's spiritual life. Some achieve this through meditation, clean living, and the study of spiritual awareness. Others might also practice witchcraft, among other spiritual techniques. Other pagans simply revere the earth, the sun, the moon, the stars, and space, as being a simply tremendous expression of God's creativity.

Common misconception: "Witchcraft and magic are evil."

Not true. Take this example: Some Christians say that anger is an evil emotion, yet the Bible describes their God as "an angry God." Or think about this: Some people blindly accept the concept that taking medicine to cure disease is a good thing, yet more and more medicines are proven harmful every day. There are no absolute black-and-white good-or-evil definitions in life. Everything and everyone contains a balance of what we call good and evil.

In years gone by, before the witch-hunts, witch trials, and inquisitions, almost every rural village had a witch who was its doctor, its teacher, its midwife, its counsellor — a friend to the people. These wise men and women were known to practice arts that were not understood by the common folk, who thought of them as "witch magic." These witches brought entire communities of people into the world, raised them, kept them healthy, educated them, guided them, and cared for them. It was a position of great responsibility. Those witches were no more evil than any of us — and that includes you. Their craft was no more evil than the work of a modern-day midwife, doctor, teacher, or policeman. Of course, even doctors, teachers, and policemen can have evil intentions sometimes — and so, too, can a witch, but it is very much the exception rather than the rule!

Common misconception: "Pagans hate or oppose the Church."

Not true. They just don't believe all the same things. Some parts of Judaism, Christianity, and Islam can be embraced by paganism, while other parts must be rejected due to their claims of infallibility and absoluteness. Pagans believe there are very few absolutes in Creation — just a balance of opposites, in a strange kind of coexistent harmony.

Common misconception: "Pagans are headed for hell."

Pagans don't acknowledge the Jewish/Christian concepts of heaven and hell. You can't go somewhere that does not exist. Hell and heaven exist only in the minds and beliefs of Christians, Jews, and Muslims. A more common pagan belief is Samadhi — which is a new state of consciousness in which the individual is entirely at one with the whole of Creation.

Common misconception: "Paganism is disorganized."

Not true. A glass has some water in it. Observer "A" sees a glass that is halfway to being empty. He also sees disorganization in the pagan lifestyle. Observer "B" sees a glass that is halfway to being filled up. He is open to new possibilities and personal discoveries in the pagan lifestyle. The pagan life does not dictate any rules —just a few fundamental laws of harmonious life. "Do what you will, as long as you harm none." Unlike most "religious" belief systems, paganism doesn't tell you what to do or think. Not all pagans believe in reincarnation, but many do. Not all pagans believe that there is a literal place of paradise at the eventual end of life's journey, but many do. Not all pagans feel the need to practice witchcraft, but many do. Paganism is not a religion of the book, so individuals must explore life's possibilities for themselves and arrive at their own conclusions; they must shape their own understanding in harmony with life and creation.

WHICH PAGAN TRADITION?

Each of the many pagan traditions, or belief systems, has a right to call itself "pagan." They all fall within the same basic framework, but each of them has a different way of expressing those basic ideas and truths. The list of traditions is huge. Here are just a few of the names you'll encounter: Alexandrian, Anglo-Romany, Anglo-Saxon, Arthurian, Brezonek, Brittanic, Brythonic, Caledonii, Celtic, Creabh Ruadh, Cymri, Deborean, Druidiactos, Druidic, Dryad, Eireannach, Faery, Family, Fennian, Gaelic, Gardnerian, Hebridean, Hibernian, Irish, Kingstone, Maidenhill, Majestic, Manx, North Country, North Isles, Northern, OBOD (Order of Bards, Ovates, and Druids), Pecti-

Wita, Reformed Druids, Romano-Gaulish, Sacred Wheel, Scotia, Scottish, Shamanic, Tuatha de Danann, Ueleda, Welsh, West Country, Wicca, Wicce, Witan, Witchcraft, Wittan, or maybe even Y Tylwyth Teg. Let's take a look at a few of the more commonly encountered traditions...

The Alexandrian tradition was founded by Alexander Saunders, a well respected pagan leader who combined Anglo-Celtic and Qabalistic beliefs and rituals. It has been suggested that this style of paganism began as early as the late 15th century, when the Moors, Jews, pagans, and other non-Catholics fled from the notorious Inquisition. Many of them went to the west of Ireland — then the end of the known world! — to hide from the Inquisition, and to start a new life in relative safety.

The Anglo-Romany tradition is based on the beliefs of the nomadic Gypsy people of Britain and Ireland (commonly known as "Tinkers"). In many cases, this tradition includes some of the mystical aspects of Roman Catholicism.

The Anglo-Saxon tradition (from England) combines the original practices of the Celts with those of the Southern Witches (Teutons). Though the popular word "Wicca" is Anglo-Saxon in origin, these practitioners prefer not to be known as Wiccan. There are many different expressions of this tradition's teachings and beliefs.

The Arthurian tradition comes from Cornwall in England, and from Wales. It is based largely upon myths and legends concerning King Arthur. Each mythical figure represents a divine aspect of the gods.

The Celtic tradition is a wide and varied system coming from Celtic Gaul, western and northern England, Ireland, Wales, Scotland, Brittany, and even the Isle of Man. A number of common features can be found in all its variations, but, in general, the word "Celtic" describes a general approach rather than specific beliefs.

The Cymri tradition is the main pagan tradition of Wales. It is said to be pre-Celtic in origin, predating much of the Arthurian legend and myths (although Arthur and his court are prominent in the mythology of Cymri as it stands today).

The Druidic traditions are broadly based on the beliefs, rituals, and magic of the Celtic Druids (the Priests). There are many different versions of this tradition, often causing serious internal arguments within the pagan community.

Family traditions include those systems of practice and belief that are passed down through individual family lines, from generation to generation. A family tradition can be a part of any culture's indigenous religion.

The Gardnerian tradition, like the Alexandrian tradition, is specifically a branch of Wicca, and was founded by Gerald Gardner. In 1951, when witchcraft became a legal activity, he began writing and publishing his ideas and philosophies. He had so much impact on paganism that many other traditions have adopted his ideas as their own. Those ideas include ritual nudity, structured coven leadership, and an organized system of education and testing for new witches. There are a lot of books on Gardnerian Wicca, but look in particular for Janet and Stewart Farrar's books on its practices.

The North Isles tradition came from the Shetland and Orkney Islands of Scotland. From the start, it was influenced by the occupying Norsemen, and many Nordic festivals are still observed. Some of the regional and deity names are still identified by old Norse words.

Pecti-Wita originated before the Celts, and is best described as the beliefs and practices of the Picts, the pre-Celtic race of northern Scotland. The Picts remained at war with the invading Celts for many years before being conquered and absorbed into the expanding Celtic society.

The Scotia tradition — even though you don't see this one very often, it's still a strong part of the pagan heritage! Sadly, it is a tradition on which very little public information exists. General opinion suggests that this path rebuilds the early Milesian (human, post-Faery) belief system. Scotia was another victim of Celtic influence and absorption. It probably contained

many of the practices of the old Spanish (Iberian) pagans, but thanks to the efficiency of the Inquisition, very little is known about it!

The Shamanic tradition is a system that strives for complete harmony with nature and creation. It relies on man, beast, and elements sharing a "common heartbeat." Although technically it isn't part of the common person's view of paganism, it has been found (at least in part) in every ancient culture discovered so far.

Tuatha de Danann is from Ireland, and is rooted in the myths of the Tuatha de Danann, the final race of Faeries before the Milesian, or human, invasion of their lands. This Irish pantheon of deities covers almost all of the Irish traditions today, and is constructed largely from the legends of the Faerie folk of Ireland.

Wicca, the Anglo-Saxon term for witchcraft, meaning "wise one," has been popularized by pagan writers since the 1950s. It is a basically Anglo-Celtic system of paganism, with its most common variants being the Gardnerian and Alexandrian traditions. Many good books have been written about Wicca and are now easy to find. Authors such as Vivienne Crowley, Scott Cunningham, Dion Fortune, and Doreen Valiente can be relied upon for solid, ethical views of Wicca and witchcraft as a whole.

The Witan tradition is a strong mix of Scottish, Celtic, Pictish, and Norse traditions. Because it includes so many different beliefs, it tends to be a fairly open and unstructured path, permitting self-initiation at any stage.

The Wittan tradition comes from Ireland, and combines the best of the old Irish traditions with some of the Norse values. It is strongly rooted in Irish history, myth, and legend, embracing anything that is added with each passing generation. Because Wittans encourage growth and progress while retaining their historical beliefs, they can change with the times without diluting their tradition. Until recently, Wittan covens were rigidly structured, but modern times have led to a more open system, allowing self-initiation and even completely solitary practice.

Many of the obvious differences between the traditions have to do with their inner structures. It's no secret that, by the time Celtic civilization crumbled under the Normans and the Church, it had become a classed society with warrior and priest classes having most of the wealth (and power). The upper classes took their love of battles and social status to ridiculous extremes, enslaving their own people to fight in local wars with other sects. As the lower (enslaved) classes become more and more discontented, an unbreachable class gap appeared, making it possible for the Norman invaders to play off one regional ruler against another. Once the Normans had succeeded in turning entire towns and cities against their neighbors (and even themselves!), they simply waited for the battle to die down and then conquered both remaining armies while they were still battle-weary.

More and more, pagans are moving away from structured coven leadership toward a more equal and even democratic structure. Even the most structured traditions now have some covens that operate in more member-oriented ways, such as rotating leaderships or consensus management. You can deduce from this trend that we all have some skill or wisdom that we can teach, and something lacking that we can learn from others. Rank and status matter less now than spiritual development and unity. However, some traditions (especially the Druidic) still don't generally share this recently accepted view.

Whether or not you identify yourself as a part of any specific pagan group is up to you alone. Remember that the most common reason given for the failure of a coven or pagan group is its internal structure — in other words, politics! — and not problems with actual spiritual practices. Before you get deeply involved with a specific group or tradition, consider your feelings about structures and leaders, ranks and responsibilities. Think about how you might react if you had a disagreement with the leadership. Think also about your reasons for wanting to join any particular group or coven. Motives are always the most important aspect of any such decision.

WHAT ABOUT SORCERY?

It should be apparent that the magick of sorcery, or in fact any kind of magick at all, is an extremely powerful and potentially beneficial way of life. It is also a potentially dangerous way of life unless you take much-needed precautions! Just imagine, back when early humanity started using fire to keep warm, how many folks burned themselves. As a rule, it would only happen to each person once — although for some, perhaps it was once too often. Exactly the same applies to magick; if you want the benefit of magick, then you have to know how to handle it properly. When you get a burn, it normally heals — at worst it leaves a scar. Magick is twice as dangerous for two reasons: first, it can't easily be seen with the naked eye, and second, it works in the aethereal realm, which defines, forms, and changes the physical realm. If magick goes wrong, it won't just damage the physical world — it can have disastrous consequences for the aethereal body too.

Sorcery, like any spiritual technique, is not to be toyed with like a child's plaything. It is not to be taken lightly like some demented parlor game. Above all, it is your motives that make the biggest difference. This isn't the place to get deeply into morality or ethics or how anyone should behave toward others — or even themselves — but please do consider that magick is not a tool to pick up and put down when the mood strikes you, but a way of life that encompasses everything you do.

STEPS OF APPRENTICESHIP

Apprenticeship is simply a matter of learning from a teacher. In this case, you're the apprentice and this book is the teacher. Of course, traditionally the apprentice has only one master who teaches everything there is to know, but, in accordance with pagan practice, you're also responsible for finding your own way. Lots of people can offer you advice, but it is very important to remember that you only have to accept ideas that make sense to you, no matter how much others insist that theirs is the only valid viewpoint. That is the first (and hardest) lesson of your apprenticeship, for it means that not only do you have a wealth of teachers at your disposal but you are also your own teacher!

An apprenticeship in sorcery involves eight main stages that will automatically take place as you develop and progress. It's always nice to know what's ahead, don't you think?

The call

This is the time when you come to realize that you have an interest in magick, psychic phenomena, the supernatural, the occult, and so on.

Searching

Once you've realized that you're interested in something that's perhaps a little unusual, the next step is to search out the specific part of it that interests you. Many people turn to books for information, many to practitioners of magick. Some are lucky enough to be born into a family that can nurture them, and some just work it out bit by bit (that takes a long time — take it from one who's been there).

Researching

The word *research* actually means "to look for again" or "to reexamine." When you're searching for your specific areas of interest, lots of avenues will be open to you all at once. Depending on the strength and exactness of the call that you felt, it may turn out that the first avenues you try aren't really for you. You need to be prepared to go back to where you came from in order to try something else until you find what you've been looking for. This can apply just as much after years of apprenticeship and even mastery of a craft. Just because you've committed to one thing now doesn't mean you have to stay with that forever onwards. It's vitally important never to allow yourself to feel trapped into something because you chose it. The only thing worse than a poor decision is sticking to it.

Experimentation

For each avenue of interest that you decide to travel, you need to look closely at what you find. It's almost irresistible to experiment a little, almost like picking up a toy from a shelf to see if it squeaks the way it should. It's like tasting a good wine before you commit to buying the whole bottle. Of course, you might find that the experiment leaves you with a bitter taste, so what you have to do is try to figure out whether that's because it's not the right thing for you or because you don't know how it should taste in the first place! Most important, don't feel rushed or pressured by anything. This is the stage at which you decide what you're going to devote most of your spiritual energies to.

Initiation

The word *initiate* means "to begin" or "to set in motion." In many cases, particularly if you're working alone, this basic initiation doesn't have to be a ritual or a ceremony. The whole point of this stage is that you make a conscious decision to commit yourself — at least for the time being — to becoming an apprentice in your chosen subject. It isn't something that you need to tell the whole world about, either. You decide what you're going to do and then you do it. It's not as if you can't go back on it later (and that, by the way, is one good reason for not telling the world about it).

Apprenticeship

Apprenticeship in magick is that tricky time which lasts for...well, the rest of your life. Sorry, but there's no other way! If you're still learning, then you're still an apprentice, even if you're a particularly well experienced one. The fact that you're learning doesn't mean you'll never be a master, though. The encouraging part is that it is entirely up to you to know when you are ready for your High Initiation. That happens to be your greatest burden at this stage, too. This is the time when you need to be looking and learning at every opportunity — learning from books, people, intuition, nature, observation, emotions, dreams, experiences, ideas, inspirations, events, history, and in fact everything that you encounter in life! Try to find some new or meaningful idea, concept, or principle in everything, and then test your findings by applying them in practice. Work hard at being an apprentice and never forget that even the greatest idea is useless until it is tested and applied. During apprenticeship in many crafts (in Wicca, for example), you may find that there are several initiations that mark your progress along a predetermined path. These are helpful to others in identifying your standing within the Craft and in allowing covens or groups to establish a hierarchy or structure.

High Initiation

There are a number of names for this stage, but they are all essentially the same. This is a point at which you have learned all that you need to learn, and experienced all that you need to experience, in order to decide that you want to follow your chosen craft to its ends. This is no longer a personal commitment to yourself. In the High Initiation of every craft (often called the Third Degree initiation), you make your commitment in the presence of the Goddess or the God who officiates over it. In most cases, the initiation involves being recognized as a dedicated citizen of the Craft by both the Goddess or God and any witnesses who are present. Because of the presence of the Goddess or God, the High Initiation has to take the form of a ceremony or ritual of some kind, if only for your own protection. After this initiation you may consider yourself a master of the Craft, but don't forget that your apprenticeship continues!

THE STEPS OF APPRENTICESHIP

The Call	When you discover your interest in the craft of magick.
Searching	Searching for the specific area in which your magickal interests lie.
Researching	Making sure that you've found your area of particular interest within the Craft.
Experimentation	Finding out whether or not you're compatible with your chosen area of interest within the Craft.
Initiation	Making a conscious personal commitment to the study and practice of the Craft, and to developing your abilities within your chosen area of interest.
Apprenticeship	The time of education and growth within your area of interest. This is where your spiritual growth and understanding take root and gradually develop into knowledge, wisdom, and experience.
High Initiation	A serious commitment, not to be taken lightly, in which you vow before the very gods to live and die by the ways of the Craft into which you have been initiated, and in which you have been an apprentice.
Mastery of Magick	Mastery of magick is when you practice your craft both as a way of life and for spiritual development. It can be achieved only through sincere and earnest learning and practice, and through the application of the experience and wisdom gained during apprenticeship.

Mastery of magick?

Magick is a part of nature. It deals with the unseen forces that hold the physical realm intact and allow the wondrous thing called life to propagate and flourish. Magick is to be found at the heart of everything you see, hear, touch, smell, and taste. But be warned: Nature will not be mastered by any individual. If you want to have mastery over that which has been lovingly given to us by the Creator, your motives are questionable at best. At worst, you would be unbalanced in your approach to magick and would very soon topple yourself spiritually.

IN CONCLUSION...

The path of magickal training is a long and often tiring one, but it is ultimately fulfilling, both spiritually and physically. You'll develop skills and abilities that others around you haven't even dreamed of. You can become adept at tasks that seem humanly impossible. You can learn the wisdom and knowledge of the ancient magick users, and benefit from seeing the successes and errors of others.

Once you've reached the High Initiation stage, you can call yourself a master of magick, but be sure to be grateful for the gift of the knowledge of magick that is on loan to you. When you die, so will your lifetime of work and knowledge. It has been said that physical death is a powerful and inevitable method of ensuring that no individual can become too entrenched in his or her own misunderstanding! Paganism views death as a change from one state to another, and it may be precisely this change that prevents us from making permanent mistakes. Blessed be!

2 CHAPTER

HOW DOES SORCERY WORK?

PLANES, DIMENSIONS, AND ELEMENTS

ravity is a natural force, and it works whether you know about it or not. You can shout and complain about it, but it won't change the pull of gravity. As children, we are told about gravity when we inevitably ask an adult why we stay on the ground if the world is floating in space. At that time (hopefully), somebody will tell us that it's because of gravity. In the same way, when somebody asks me how magick makes things happen, I can only tell them that it's because of aether. More specifically, there are things — places, if you will — called aethereal planes.

Imagine a shopping mall where many shops sell different goods, but you've only been in the bookshop that is nearest to the door of the mall. One day you ask the bookshop's owner if he knows where you can buy some clothes, and he replies, "Oh, that'll be the clothes shop next door." The clothes shop has been there all along, but you've never seen it, and to get to it you just need to leave the bookshop and go through the door to the clothes shop. Now, think of the bookshop as the material world that you live in right now. You've probably never left it (if you have, then you can skip this section because you know what's coming next!). An aethereal plane is simply the shop next door, or the shop next to that, or the restaurant at the end of the mall — anywhere, in fact, but the bookshop. The reason it's called "aethereal" is because it isn't physical or material — unlike the world you know so well. Aether is basically a name that is sometimes given to the force or energy that makes up life itself. There are many other names for it, such as akasha, spirit energy, God energy, life force, chi, astral force, and even plain old ether (but that one gets confused with the chemical compound of the same name). These planes are aethereal because they have no physical component. The physical plane in which we live out our lives, however, has an aethereal component that holds the physical together and provides the life force necessary for its sustenance.

Aether is just one element of our physical existence here in this universe. There are four major physical elements that work with aether to form the basis of creation itself, in much the same way as DNA forms the building blocks for life as we know it. That makes a total of five elements, and, because we live primarily in the physical world, aether is seen as being the fifth of those elements (but it is by no means less important than the others). The four physical elements used in magick are fire, water, air, and earth. Each of them has two polarities, or states of operation: positive polarity is normally a constructive state in which energies are strengthened or increased, and negative polarity is normally a reductive state in which energies tend to be weakened or reduced.

The element of fire
Fire is associated with heat and with expansion. Its color is red. In the Tarot, it is associated with the suit of Swords. In its positive state, it is normally constructive and creative. In its negative state, it is destructive, dissecting, and all-consuming.

The element of water
Water is associated with coldness and with shrinkage. Its color is blue. In the Tarot, it is associated with the suit of Cups. In its positive state, it is normally nourishing, life-giving, and protective. In its negative state, it is normally fermenting, dividing, enveloping, and dissecting.

The element of air
Air is closely related to both fire and water, and is able to keep balanced between the positive and negative activities of both. Its color is yellow. In the Tarot, it is associated with the suit of Wands. Air contains a balance between the dryness of fire and the humidity of water. In its positive state it is sustaining, forceful, and feeds the fire element. In its negative state it is suffocating, stagnating, and extinguishes the fire element.

The element of earth

Earth is closely related to air, fire, and water, as it encompasses them all in its solid form. Its color is green. In the Tarot, it is associated with the suit of Pentacles. The general properties of earth are heaviness, closeness, and solidity.

The human body contains all four of the elements because it is a scaled-down model of the universe (or cosmos, if you like). Your body and aetheric energies are easily influenced by the cosmos and, believe it or not, your body and energies can in turn influence the cosmos. If you have some form of disharmony in your body, it turns up in the form of sickness. If your body is in good harmony, it shows up in your health, strength, and vitality (some even say it influences good looks, but that doesn't seem to have worked all that well for me).

Tradition from the Old Religion onwards makes it clear that you can divide your body up into four elemental sections. The feet, legs, and bowels relate to the earth element; the abdomen relates to the water element; the chest relates to the air element; and the hands, arms, shoulders, neck, and head relate to the fire element.

PROPERTIES OF THE ELEMENTS

	FIRE	**WATER**	**AIR**	**EARTH**
Color	Red	Blue	Yellow	Green
Tarot	Swords	Cups	Wands	Pentacles
Positive	Constructive, creative	Protective, nourishing, life-giving	Sustaining, forceful, feeds fire	Solid, dependable, stable
Negative	Destructive, dissecting, consuming	Dividing, fermenting enveloping, dissecting	Suffocating stagnating, infiltrating	Obstructive burdening, choking
Body	Arms, neck, shoulders, and head	Abdomen	Chest	Feet, legs, and bowels

The mind and the heart are associated specifically with the aether element as well. This is very important for users of magick of any kind, because an imbalance of any element may cause unexpected results (if you're lucky, you simply won't get a result).

All five elements are neatly tied together for you in the sign of the pentagram, which is a perfect expression of the balance and unity of the five elements. It also fits the image of the human form and expresses our relationship with Creation itself. For this reason, the pentagram (or pentacle) is an ancient sign of salutation to the Goddess and God, and to elemental forces.

But back to the shopping mall for a moment... Did you know that there are other shopping malls, too? These other malls are known as dimensions. Simply put, they are alternate realities that can be reached and seen via the aethereal realm. There's no need to think too deeply about these now because you'll come to understand their significance later on, but it is helpful to realize that they're there (although where "there" is could be anyone's guess!).

WHO FEEDS THE MAGICK?

This, the smallest question, has the biggest answer. Who, or what, is feeding the magick when it's at work? The answer is that it depends on what kind of magick you're talking about. Magick can be subdivided into three distinct groups as far as power supply is concerned.

Originator-powered

This is where, for example, a spell is cast by a sorcerer. The spell is powered by energy raised and provided by the sorcerer in person. As long as it is the sorcerer's will to continue the spell, and as long as the sorcerer is able to provide the energy for it, the spell will continue to work until it is completed. A good example is a spell of spiritual protection that is cast to protect others while they undertake a task that could place them at the mercy of other spiritual entities. In this case, recipients of the spell would not be able to rely on their own ability to protect themselves!

Recipient-powered

Here the magick is kept alive by the recipients of the spell, whether intentionally or not. Any energy or thought forms required for the spell are created by (or drawn from) the recipients of the spell. Two obvious examples spring to mind, the first being the classic "voodoo curse" in which recipients fuel the curse through their own fear and belief, and the second being a form of semi-hypnotic suggestion where recipients are aided in their goals by simply believing what they are told by the magick user. In either case, should the recipients cease believing in the magick, it would stop working immediately.

Self-sustaining

These enchantments are tricky to set up but, if done correctly, are able to sustain themselves indefinitely until they are specifically broken. The idea is simple enough: first, you set up an environment or an object into which the magick can be focused and kept. This could be anything from a pebble to an entire geographical region, though more common applications include charms, jewelry, amulets, ornaments, magickal tools, weapons, potions, powders, and various keepsakes. The enchantment is made, either providing enough aetheric energy for the lifetime of the spell or providing a blessing that enables an external source of energy to feed it. The magickal energy is then symbolically bound into the object or area and it becomes self-sustaining. A classic example of this is the wax doll, which is used as an aethereal homing device! It is enchanted in the name of the person whom it represents and then whatever happens to the doll will happen to that person as well. Of course, you must realize that to touch another with magick without their permission and knowledge is what witches would call black magick — a slippery slope indeed!

There is one other category that is really a subdivision of this one, which is Elementally sustained magick. This is a similar idea except that you can either ask for (but not necessarily receive) the help of an Elemental being (a fire spirit, a water spirit, an air spirit, or an earth spirit) or you can create — out of your own body energies — an Elementary being. Elementary beings must be created with extreme caution because, although they are separate from you, they draw power from their creator (in the same way that you draw power from your Creator). They are limited to your lifetime, because without you they cannot draw power. They pose a risk of unbalancing your own body energies and elements, because you have no control over their function beyond your initial spell. You need to construct them very carefully so that they cannot be manipulated by others, and so that they will cease

MAGICK'S ENERGY SOURCES

Originator-powered magick
The spell is powered directly by the sorcerer.

Recipient-powered magick
The spell is powered by the subject's own belief, often due to fear, strong emotions, or hypnotic or semi-hypnotic suggestion.

Self-sustained magick
A specific object or area is magickally bound with a self-contained spell, which has enough power to sustain itself during its specified lifetime.

Elementally sustained magick
A specific object or area is made into a magickal domain (dwelling place) for a cooperating Elemental spirit being (or an Elementary spirit being created from the sorcerer's own energy). The spirit can then sustain the magick.

functioning if you are jeopardized by them. When their usefulness has expired, you must deconstruct them just as carefully — to just terminate them would be like pulling a hose-pipe from the water supply without turning off the water first.

So magick comes in lots of shapes and sizes and forms, and each spell needs a power source — some for a long time and others for only a predetermined fixed duration.

EXAMPLES OF MAGICKAL VARIETIES

As you might have already gathered, a number of different factors have to be taken into consideration when you're going use magick for any reason. Some of the factors to consider will be governed by where you are at the time, some by how much time and freedom you have in which to prepare, others by the effect that is needed, and some by the intended subject or target of the magick.

Some magick may need to be worked by you alone, perhaps even in secret, while other magick may need assistance from somebody else. If you're working alone that's called Solitary magick, but if you're being helped or protected by somebody else it's Assisted magick. Sometimes you may find that a ritual, ceremony, or a visual dramatic representation of the magick is needed, in which case that would be Enacted magick. Other times you'll find that you can do almost everything necessary in your mind (or by singing, speaking, or chanting), which is Envisioned magick. Some magick changes, moves, or affects people, objects, or events and is called Active magick, while other magick involves looking for, seeing, predicting, or divining information (or images) and is called Divinatory magick.

Then there's the point of ethics that was mentioned earlier (you remember, the one I said we wouldn't go into too deeply). If the magick you intend to do is honorable and keeps within the Sorcerer's Code and the Wiccan Rede, then it can safely be considered White magick. If not, then you're talking about Black magick, and you need to be aware that you could be placing yourself in very real danger if you continue down that road (not that you would, I'm sure).

In addition, there are some general categories into which all magick falls, one way or the other. You don't really need to make any conscious decisions about the categories, because they just fall into place on their own. They are dictated by the nature of the magick you're considering, by the end result that you want to achieve, and by the way in which you hope to achieve that result.

Magick that acts primarily on the physical plane is known as Low magick — not because it isn't as powerful or important as aethereal magick — but because in terms of psychic harmonics, anything physical has a much lower (more basic) vibrational field than anything aethereal. The opposite, High magick, acts mainly on the aethereal plane and normally does not manifest much physical evidence of its actions. Oddly, people who don't understand the difference between High and Low magick seem to be more easily impressed by Low magick, because they can see its effects with their own eyes.

At the same time, your magick can be created by either a Shadow or an Enchantment. In general terms, an Enchantment is simply a spell that is spoken, written, or even thought (or willed) into existence. A Shadow spell is one that is formed by a kind of magickal template — such as a ritual, a dance, a ceremony, a magickally charged tool or image, or even by pictorial symbology. Consequently, Enchantments are most often classified as Envisioned magick while shadows are most often classified as Enacted magick (although there are exceptions to every rule!).

The last thing to determine is whether your magick is Natural (also called Small) or Supernatural (also called Arcane) magick. This is determined by the intended action and method of your magick. Natural magick is the kind that witches commonly employ, which stays firmly within the bounds of commonly accepted laws of nature and physics (without bending too many of them, anyway). Supernatural magick (and that does not mean "paranormal," by the way) is just the opposite: it appears to break natural and physical laws — although this is often simply because our knowledge of science hasn't advanced sufficiently to understand why it seems that way. Don't forget that the aethereal realm is not governed by the same physical laws and properties as the physical realm in which we live. If you change something significantly in the aethereal plane, which parallels our physical plane, the physical plane will try to follow suit regardless of whether or not our natural and physical laws allow! Perhaps the most useful law of magickal essence is simply this: "As above, so below." "Above" means the aethereal plane, and "below" means the physical. It is saying simply that the physical realm generally imitates the aethereal, even if it takes some time to achieve the changes.

SOLITARY OR ASSISTED MAGICK?

When you come to decide whether you want to work magick with assistance or cooperation from somebody else, there are a few things you'll need
to consider. First: How much power does the magick need, and can you
handle it effectively alone? If not, you'll need help from another magick
user. Second: Can you safely cast the magick on your own or would it be
wiser to have somebody else present in case things go wrong? If you can't
guarantee your own safety, you'd be sensible to ask another magickally com-
petent associate to stand by just in case. Third: Would the magick be any
more effective if lots more power were thrown at it? If that would help, you
could consider taking your cause to brothers and sisters in the Craft and
asking for their cooperation — after you make sure they understand the
objectives and don't have any problem with your motives or goal. Fourth: Is
there some physical or practical limitation that demands more than one person's being present for the casting or maintenance of the magick? If, for
example, you wanted to use magick to start a car that had run out of fuel,
you'd probably be wanting to push-start it. It wouldn't be easy to concentrate on the magick while simultaneously trying to push the car, steer it, and
coordinate the gears. Time to call in some practical help, but even better, an
extra magick user who can work on the magick at the same time.

The only warning about assisted or cooperative magick is that what you
gain in power and concentration, you risk losing in control. When there are
two or more minds working on the same magick at the same time, they need
to be in complete and total harmony. That makes it very difficult to alter the
course of the magick if you sense the need to do so during the casting. Every
mind involved has to "own" the goal of the magick and be absolutely focused
on it in fine detail. If one person in the group has a slightly different view of
what's meant to happen, the magick may not work at all. Of course, that isn't
an issue when there's only one of you. You have to decide whether or not the
benefits outweigh the disadvantages every single time you cast some magick.

ACTION OR DIVINATION?

Everything you choose to do, whether physically or magickally, either affects
something or observes something. Either you're watching something that

exists and develops on its own, or you're affecting, changing, or influencing something. I concede that you might be able to think of one or two things that don't fit either category, but it's a general rule that fits almost everything in life. Either you're doing or you're observing. It's worth noting that not all observation is done with the eyes. You can observe just as easily with any of your five physical senses or, magickally speaking, with your sixth sense — that is, your psychic abilities. We all have psychic abilities, but not all of us know how to recognize when we're using them.

Your magick will normally be put to use for a specific purpose, to fulfill a specific task. Sometimes that task involves finding something out or looking for something, perhaps searching for a missing person or finding lost property, maybe even locating spirits or energy sources. That's Divinatory magick.

One very important thing you need to know before you start is that the aethereal realm isn't limited by time in the same way that the physical realm is, although the results you get inevitably are filtered by time as they bridge across into the physical realm where you see or sense them. For that reason, it is vital that you know roughly to what time period your divination relates. Sadly, the future is the hardest of all to see, because it fluctuates wildly with changing possibilities in every moment that passes. Sometimes you can see the future quite clearly and it turns out exactly the way you saw it, because you happened to see the version of the future that coincided with the way events actually took place. Sometimes you might see a future that simply never happens because events turned and deviated before time reached the point you saw. Just thinking about that can really mess around with your mind, so please don't lose too much sleep over that one! Needless to say, the past is already fixed and so should be fairly easy to divine. The present is simply the wet concrete that will shortly be the hardened pavement of the past, so that's pretty simple too. The present is where the possibilities of the future turn into the realities of the past, and so it takes a very fluid shape. That could be important because the results that you divine one minute may not be true a moment later. In other words, if you're divining in the present tense, check and recheck your results if there's any possibility that circumstances might change.

Sometimes the task at hand will involve doing something rather than just finding things out. That's Active magick. The task may be a simple matter of influencing the possibilities for the future to make an event happen in a specific way in the present, and finally turn into a "done deal" in the past. The task may be more complex and involve actually changing the way things are already happening, or even altering the end result of things that have already happened. That's a lot of theoretical time-sensitive jargon though, isn't it?

Here's an example. My first task is simple: I'll try to make the person at the front of the ice-cream line forget what he wanted so he'll go away and think about it, thus moving me one place closer to the ice-cream vendor. The future possibility is that the person at the front may or may not forget what he wanted — or may or may not order a load of ice cream and take ages! By magick, then, I would simply try to influence that possibility in my favor. I should point out that anyone who actually does this is seriously wasting spiritual energies...

Now my second task is more complex: I want to get home, but the road ahead is flooded out. In this case, there's no chance of the water's suddenly draining away or evaporating, so I would have to change the result of a past event, causing the water go away by sorcery. Alternatively, I could go for the long shot and try to give people with mobile water pumps a strong desire to visit the stretch of road I'm on, but you've got to keep a sense of realism, too. Use what you've got and what is most likely to work. Some magickal purists will say that you should be able to do almost anything using sorcery alone — but why should you use sorcery if there's a less demanding way that's more easily arranged? In the first case, the ultimately simple method would be to cut in at the front of the ice-cream line and risk getting thumped. In the second case, it might be to turn the car around and try a different road. A good sorcerer is always practical and sensible.

Magick is not often restricted by geography, and, as you've seen already, it can certainly break the time barrier if you treat that privilege with care. Because all magick works on the aethereal plane — even if it's working on the physical plane as well — it can transcend distance and time. That means your spell can operate in any place, at any time. That's useful to know when your brother falls ill in deepest, darkest Peru and you're stuck in Peoria. There's no way you can physically get to him to heal him, so what do you do? Get yourself a witness of him (something that represents him) that you can use as a focus for your healing magick (in a pinch, even envisioning him in your mind is sufficient). Cast your magick on the witness and the deed is done. No time lag — distance no object! By the way, anything personal can act as a witness for anybody or anything. For example, you could use a photo, a lock of hair, or even somebody's signature. When you think about it hard enough, that's a bit worrying. What powers are you actually giving to complete strangers every time you write out a personal check or sign a credit agreement? What about when somebody takes your photograph? Many tribal cultures still hold that photographs "steal your soul," and the daunting part is that they're right! You could become quite paranoid about that, but there are plenty of magickal protections available if it becomes a concern for you.

ENACTMENT OR ENVISIONMENT?

The quickest way to cast your magick is, without doubt, Envisionment, in which you simply visualize, speak, chant, wish, or even sing the spell into being. There are a few reasons why you may prefer not to do that though. First: it isn't always safe, because there's no easy way of setting up solid spiritual protection without physically defining a safe location in which to work your magick, and for that you'd normally need a ritual or ceremony of some kind. Second: you may need to coordinate with other people who don't know the spell you're using, in which case you'd need to teach them first — and time or circumstances may not permit that. Third: you may prefer to use a ritual to raise power for the spell, or to strengthen the image and effectiveness of the spell in the mind of its recipient (and consequently his or her belief in it).

There are also reasons why you might prefer to use Envisioned magick instead of ritual or ceremonial magick. First: you may already be inside the confines of a magickally protected place (such as a magick circle) and have all the power and safety you need. Second: you may be experienced enough to know with certainty that the spell doesn't need any form of outward expression in order to work effectively. Third: it may be that your surroundings, circumstances, or the time available prevents you from casting any other kind of magick. Think about casting a headache-banishing spell while sitting on the train traveling home after a hard day at the office. I'm betting you don't have your athame (see page 66) with you, and that even if you do you wouldn't want to use it in public, right?

The opposite of Envisioned magick is Enacted magick, which is simply any magick that you cast with an outward expression such as a ritual, a ceremony, or even an reenactment of some significant event.

Such expressions are very powerful because they act as a mold for the magick, a form upon which the magick can be built and which keeps it steady and true long after it is cast and put out of your mind. Any enactment forms a solid impression on the mind of anyone who notices it. Think about your favorite television films — how many of them can you not remember the ending of? How many can you not remember the general plot of? How many do you not remember the central characters of?

Varieties of Magick

SOLITARY OR ASSISTED?

Solitary Magick

The sorcerer works alone and unaided, often in secret. This method is often the most convenient and also least complicated. It also offers less protection.

Assisted Magick

Two or more sorcerers or magick users work together to achieve a spell. They can protect each other and raise more energy than when they are working alone.

ACTIVE OR DIVINATION?

Active

The magick changes, moves, or somehow affects the subject of the spell (for example, people, places, objects, or events).

Divination

The magick helps the sorcerer to see, look for, predict, or find out something specific about people, places, objects, or events.

ENACTED OR ENVISIONED?

Enacted Magick

The magick is brought into being by means of a ritual, ceremony, or other visual representation. This helps to focus the minds of all involved.

Envisioned Magick

The magick is brought into being by thinking, speaking, chanting, or singing. It is often the quickest method, but also requires well-developed mental concentration abilities.

If an enactment makes any impression on your mind at all, it tends to be a very complete and detailed one. A lot of it comes down to your own preferences and natural aptitude for the dramatic. Sometimes you might use an enactment for the benefit of your own mind — sometimes for other people's benefit. In some cases, such as the casting of a protective magick circle, it's just a plain necessity — there's simply no other practical way of doing it!

PSYCHIC ENHANCEMENTS

Some people describe themselves as "psychic" because they have intuitive feelings about people or events that often turn out to be correct. They're actually stating the obvious through a slight misunderstanding. Once again, turning to my dictionary for assistance, the word "psychic" is derived from the root word "psych," which in turn is derived from the Greek word *psukhe*. These words all refer to the mind's processes — to thought itself. To be psychic is to have thoughts. If you don't have at least that much functionality in your mind, you're technically brain-dead and have no right to be reading books! What those people mean is that they exhibit some unusual psychic abilities. Some people call them "psychic powers," which is perhaps more accurate. The psychic enhancement of magick is simply the ability to use the inherent power of the human mind to increase the effectiveness of the magick being used. It offers a way for magick to break through otherwise impenetrable mental and aethereal barriers. You will find more about the psychic enhancement of magick in the Psychic Enhancement chapter later in this book.

3 CHAPTER
SORCERY'S REASONS
AND SEASONS

THE SORCERER'S CODE AND THE LAW OF RETURN

At some point you're going to have to consider why you're casting magick. What are your reasons and motives? What are your goals along the way? Who or what is going to benefit from your use of that which the Creator has given you? This book isn't about moral standards, but it is concerned with ethics. You do need to establish ground rules and stick with them, modifying them along the way if you find that you need to. The rules that your ethics dictate will be governed by the moral standards by which you already live your life, so don't try to be something that you aren't already — unless it is your lifetime goal to change!

Speaking as one who has been around magickal influences for a fair length of time, I could tell you pretty concisely where my ethics lie, what I am happy to do and what I would never dream of doing...but I won't. Every pagan has to find his or her own path. There are, however, two vitally important things for which you need to set your policies immediately. First, you must decide whether or not you will ever accept payment for your magickal services. Second, you must decide whether or not you will ever be willing to cross the line between White and Black magick for any reason at all. Set these policies carefully and never go back on them — they will determine your magickal character and makeup as a sorcerer. As a rough guide, traditional witches and sorcerers do not charge fees, but will accept gifts that are offered freely and out of gratitude after the magick has been cast. Traditionally, you will also find that Black magick is considered taboo — which is from the Tongan word *tabu,* meaning socially or spiritually unacceptable.

There are two things that, as a sorcerer, you will do well to keep in mind at all times during the planning, preparation, and casting of magick. The first is the Wiccan Rede, which is the traditional witches' code of ethics. The second is the Sorcerer's Code, which embodies the ethics by which sorcerers have lived and worked for many centuries. Here, then, is the Wiccan Rede:

Bide the Wiccan law ye must,
In perfect love, in perfect trust.
Eight words the Wiccan Rede fulfil:
An ye harm none, do what ye will.
What ye send forth comes back to thee,
So ever mind the Rule of Three.
Follow this with mind and heart,
And merry ye meet, and merry ye part.

Next, the Sorcerer's Code:

Within the sorcerer there lies both man and beast:
Let not the beast's hunger set aside the man's wisdom,
Let not the beast be indulged of the magick of sorcery.
Forsake not this most sacred of codes
Lest ye be struck by deeds of your own making.

A gift before a service is an ill-disguised bribe.
Work not at anyone who has not requested magick.
Fury surely plays folly with both truth and wisdom.
As ye plant, so shall ye harvest three-fold and more.

Consequences are as inescapable as the winter's coming.
Follow the Craft and live beyond reproach in the world.

Courage and Honor are to be sought and maintained.
Friendship is given without price or thought of return.
Show dignity, grace, and favor to all who come to you.
Secrecy is of either Honor or Deceit; know which it is.
Knowledge is a wage to share with fellow laborers.

Keep safe the Craft's secrets from Initiation until death.
Speak ill of nobody, alive or beyond the veil.
In all that you do be honest and true without exception.
This above all: to thine own self be true.

Those are pretty strongly worded codes of ethics. They've been put together, perfected, and passed down for thousands of years for good reason. Without a code of ethics such as the Sorcerer's Code or the Wiccan Rede, you could end up in a conflict-of-interests situation with no definite ground rules to govern your behavior. In cases like that, you would normally be under pressure and (quite humanly) liable to make errors of judgment that you would later regret!

A common thread runs through both those codes of ethics: the Law of Three-Fold Return. There is no major religious belief system in the world today that does not have some form of three-fold-return law. Some of them have even increased the rather symbolic number to seven or even ten to really press the point home. The law, at its simplest, is best quoted as "you reap what you sow." The reason it is so popular in religion as a whole is that it is an inescapable truth. In some cases, it may appear that somebody has "got away with it" when they commit a crime, but you can be sure that somewhere down the line, they'll get stung for it. It's not that there's a huge judge sitting in the sky who punishes people; it's more like a self-governing system. If you think about it, nobody controls gravity, and yet everything that comes into contact with it is affected by it. It's your own spiritual track record that eventually pins you down. If you spend a lot of time doing unethical things, then your spiritual (aetheric) vibrational energies will naturally begin to resonate with similar things, and we all know that similar vibrational energies harmonize and attract each other. The same goes for thinking about and doing positive and ethical things — you'll harmonize with those good things, and there's your law of return. It's absolutely unavoidable, and that is why you have to set your sights high when you set your personal standards and ethics.

This effect is sometimes known as Karma or the Law of Cause and Effect. Either way it is rooted in the aetheric realm, so it tends not to regard either time or geography. Remember that physicists for years have stuck to the rule: "For every action there is an equal and opposite reaction." Every single deed of ours, including those on the aethereal level (which includes thoughts, by the way!) has a cause that triggers it and a result that follows it sooner or later (sometimes much later). For everything you do, a reaction will come back to you in order to keep the aether balanced. That's a universal (cosmic) system in action, and there's nothing you can do to stop it. The balancing-out might come in an instant, in a few minutes, in a few hours, days, weeks, months, years, or even lifetimes — but it will come eventually. The most important lesson you can draw from this immutable law is not only that you are responsible for your own actions, but that caution is a virtue, because you will eventually pay for the mistakes you make along the way.

THE WHITE (BENEVOLENT) AND THE BLACK (MALEVOLENT)

White or Black magick? It isn't always absolutely obvious which is which. Here's an example: Your sister tells you that your brother-in-law has been taken ill and is in a very serious condition, and that the hospital is holding him for observation until further notice. You know perfectly well that a little healing magick would work wonders for him, but your sister doesn't want you to get involved. You're sure you could relieve the pain completely and put him on the road to good health again in a matter of hours. There are two arguments that you might consider. First, the magick would obviously be White magick because it's healing, it's constructive, and it's returning things to their normal state. Right? Second, the magick would obviously be Black magick because you'd be interfering with someone else's life without his permission. What if he's ill because he's on the receiving end of some huge karmic principle? If you were to cure the illness for him, that karma would still be lurking around the next corner for him!

The whole point of the difference between White and Black magick is realizing that you don't always know what's best. You might think you do, or even be utterly convinced that you do, but you don't. None of us can possibly know what's best for anyone else in the grand, eternal, universal scheme of things. The only person who has a right to decide how your life is managed is you, and the same applies to everyone else as well. In this particular case, I'd have to call your intervention Black magick — even though that sounds a little melodramatic.

Consider this example, though. You know a nice old lady who has a nice little dog that's very dear to her. One day the dog goes out for its usual stroll around the garden, but fails to come back when she calls it. When you visit her that afternoon she is obviously upset and can't understand why her dog won't come back inside. You take a look in the yard and see that it probably escaped through a hole in the fence. You have a choice to make now: you could use a little divinatory magick, perhaps a little psychically enhanced mirror-gazing, or you could just try your best to comfort her while offering to help organize a search party. The argument for the divination's being Black magick is that she hasn't asked you to use magick to find the dog. The argument for the divination's being White magick is that she's lost a dog and you know you can find it with your skills as a seer. What are you to do?

There is actually no specifically correct answer. It seems to be primarily the dog that has the problem (being lost, that is) and there's no way you could get permission from a dog to use magick on its behalf. On the other hand, it may be a lesson that the old lady has to learn before her life is over — perhaps a lesson about being able to let go of worldly or emotional attachments? However, there's always the chance that the dog is going to come to harm if it stays lost, so maybe finding it quickly would be the best thing to do. In this case I'd be quite happy for my students to choose either option, provided that their motive for doing so was good, honorable, and well-intentioned. Of course, you still have to consider that the Law of Return doesn't judge you on your motives — it just happens to you if it needs to!

THE LOW (PHYSICAL) AND THE HIGH (AETHEREAL)

Low magick and High magick are slightly misleading names. As we've seen before, their titles seem to imply that one is somehow greater or more impressive than the other, but that isn't true. In fact, you'll probably find that Low magick is considerably more appealing to the uninitiated, because it does things that you can see, hear, smell, touch, or taste. It appeals to the most base, materialistic, and physical mind because it bends rules that have always seemed unbendable. Low magick is the physical magick that sorcerers use to alter physical surroundings, objects, events, or appearances. Sometimes those alterations are permanent and other times they may be intended to be illusionary (known as apparitions), for only a particular period of time. Low magick is closely akin to what some call telekinesis or psychokinesis, the apparent ability to move physical objects using only the power of one's mind. There is a popular argument within the Craft that most of the psychic phenomena experienced in the world today are executed by people who have magickal skills without understanding the processes they are going through.

Low magick manifestly affects things on the physical plane, but it also affects the aethereal plane around us. Remember that the physical plane is held together by the aethereal plane that is its counterpart.

If, in the aethereal realm, you change something that has a physical-realm counterpart, you can expect the physical counterpart to try to catch up sooner or later. In the case of healing magick, it's obviously hoped that the physical will heal sooner rather than later. On the other hand, if you're strengthening a tree for healthy growth, the physical should catch up slowly as the tree grows up. Either way, the physical realm always tries to balance itself out with its aethereal counterpart, and the old saying "Nature will find a way" always proves itself true eventually. As above, so below.

High magick is the kind of magick that takes place purely in the aethereal realm without manifestly affecting the physical. That doesn't mean that the results of the magick won't have effects that are visible in the physical world — just that the magick itself doesn't directly alter the physical realm. Most High magick is purely spiritual, elemental, energy-altering, or God-force oriented. This is the kind of magick where your own spiritual protection becomes an issue, because you'll be dealing with forces, energies, and perhaps even spirits over which you don't have any guaranteed control. Caution is always advised when working High magick of any kind, even if it seems simple to begin with!

THE SHADOW (RITUAL) AND THE ENCHANTMENT (SPELL)

The word "shadow" can give the wrong impression. When referring to Shadow magick, it doesn't mean dark, sinister, secretive, hidden, or unseen. A shadow is just a basic outline of something more permanent — a rough blueprint of something that can be created later on. Most often this takes the form of an enacted ritual or ceremony in which the words, the actions, and even the drama help the minds of those involved to understand and form the magick. It is very important to be aware that it isn't the shadow itself that creates, or even defines, the magick, because that would imply that anyone could just pick up a script of a ritual and it would all start happening as the words were spoken. From experience, I can tell you that that doesn't happen at all. The people involved in a ritual still need to understand what it is they're doing and how it's going to affect the aethereal and physical realms; they need to be magickally trained (or at least aware) in order to be able to raise and manipulate the energy that the magick needs. The people provide the energy, the will, and the direction, while the shadow provides the magick with an overall shape and the people with a common focus.

Lots of magick can be cast without the use of a shadow ritual or ceremony because once you know the intended "shape" of the magick in your mind, it simply takes form according to your will. If your mind is trained well enough to be able to shape the magick and keep its focus while simultaneously concentrating on raising energy and directing it, why not do so? That's known as an Enchantment, or Spell. (By the way, the result of a Shadow is also a Spell, but is normally known as a Shadow, so that there's no ambiguity as to how the magick was created.) The biggest temptation is to view Enchantments as "easy magick," because they don't appear to need any preparation, equipment, or scripts. Sadly, that isn't true at all. You need just as much preparation — and sometimes even a script — if it's a long Enchantment that you haven't yet committed to memory. The preparation might not involve gathering together physical components and equipment, but it involves all the same ideas, concepts, symbology, visual imagery, and structure. In other words, it isn't a shortcut — it's actually the long way around. In almost all Enchantments you need a strong mind for visualization of goals, and you must be able to stay focused no matter what happens around you.

In preparing for an Enchantment, you may find it useful to write your aim or goal in your personal Book of Shadows and Enchantments. Also draw out, or describe in written form, any visual imagery or symbology you want to use. Finally write out the actual words of the Enchantment when you're happy that you've got them just right.

THE SMALL (NATURAL) AND THE ARCANE (SUPERNATURAL)

The proper name for natural magick is Small magick, while supernatural magick is known as Arcane magick. In much the same way as Low and High magick, the terms Small and Arcane tend to imply that one is somehow

Magickal Classifications

WHITE OR BLACK MAGICK?

White Magick

White magick is that which is benevolent, either intentionally or otherwise. It does good, not harm. Magick without the subject's permission is seldom classed as white.

Black Magick

Black magick is that which is malevolent, either intentionally or otherwise. It does harm to the subject. Magick used without the subject's permission is normally classed as black.

LOW OR HIGH MAGICK?

Low Magick

Low magick relates to the physical realm (the realm in which we live).

High Magick

High magick relates to the aethereal realms of spiritual and elemental life.

SHADOW OR ENCHANTMENT?

Shadow Magick

Shadow magick is that which is created using a ritual, or a series of actions. It is often cast while under some form of magickal protection.

Enchantment Magick

Enchantment magick refers to spells that are created by thinking, speaking, chanting, or singing (sometimes in conjunction with magickal charms, tools, or rituals).

SMALL OR ARCANE?

Small Magick

Small magick refers to natural magick (which operates strictly within the commonly accepted laws of nature and physics).

Arcane Magick

Arcane magick refers to supernatural magick (which does not conform to the commonly accepted laws of nature and physics).

superior to the other. That is not true. The terms Low and High are a way of describing how the magick will work. The terms Small and Arcane are a way of describing what the magick will affect.

Small magick works within the commonly accepted laws of nature and physics, which means that the definition of Small magick may change with man's understanding of nature and physics! Arcane magick reaches outside those accepted boundaries. It is perfectly possible for magick to be both Small and Arcane at the same time, affecting both the natural and the supernatural. These aren't so much cut-and-dried classifications as a sliding scale that helps to describe where the majority of the magick's action lies.

There is, perhaps not surprisingly, a very strong correlation between Small magick and Low magick, because both operate within the commonly accepted natural and physical world. That does not mean, however, that they are the same thing. It is possible to have magick that is High and Small — for example, a spell that encourages healing in accordance with the human body's own health mechanisms. Magick can be Low and Arcane — for example, a spell that physically moves an object from one place to another (also sometimes known as telekinesis).

THE SEASONS OF THE YEAR (THE SABBATS)

It's also important to understand the significance of changing times and seasons in improving the effectiveness of both your magickal workings and your spiritual life. Every year there are eight commonly observed pagan sabbats, which mark the changes of seasons and astronomical events. There are four Lesser Sabbats (Spring Equinox, Midsummer, Autumn Equinox, and Yule) interspersed with the four Greater Sabbats (Candlemas, Beltane, Lammas, and Samhain). Of course, the sabbats are not the only seasons of the year. They are separated by periods of approximately six weeks each. These correlate to signs of the zodiac, times of day, the cycle of spiritual life, moon phases, directions, planets, and even sun phases.

The chart shown on the next page describes the relationships between these different factors. In addition, associated with each sabbat are different dates, colors, magickal tools and equipment, energies, goddesses, gods, rituals, spells, and customs. It is useful in celebrating the sabbats to know

The Cycle of the Year

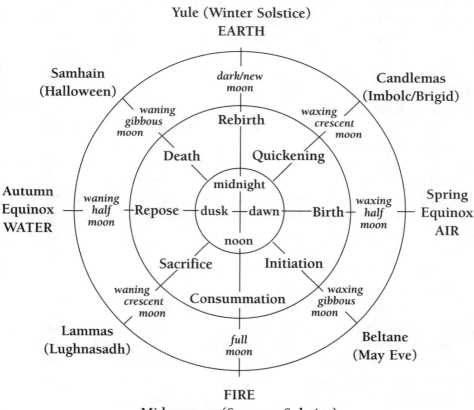

Yule (Winter Solstice)
EARTH

Samhain (Halloween)

Candlemas (Imbolc/Brigid)

dark/new moon

waning gibbous moon

waxing crescent moon

Rebirth

Death   Quickening

midnight

Autumn Equinox WATER

waning half moon

Repose — dusk — dawn — Birth

waxing half moon

Spring Equinox AIR

noon

Sacrifice   Initiation

waning crescent moon

Consummation

waxing gibbous moon

Lammas (Lughnasadh)

full moon

Beltane (May Eve)

FIRE
Midsummer (Summer Solstice)

which of these you can use to help you capture the true meaning of each one, and to help make your magickal works all the more effective. Here is a listing of the eight sabbats in their chronological order throughout the year.

Candlemas

Also called Imbolc, Oimelc, Brigid, Brigid's Day, or Groundhog Day, and has merged with Lupercalia (Valentine's Day). Dates covered are around February 2nd and early February (as late as February 14th). Associated colors are white and red. Tools to use are candles, seeds, the Brigid wheel, and milk. Energies involved are conception, initiation, and inspiration. Associated goddesses are Brigid and the Maiden. Associated gods are the Groundhog and any other creatures emerging from hibernation. Appropriate rituals include creative inspiration, purification, initiation, candle work, house and temple blessings. Common customs include lighting candles, seeking the signs of spring, housecleaning, and welcoming Brigid.

Spring Equinox

Also called Ostara, St. Patrick's Day, and Easter. Dates covered are around March 21st. Associated colors are green and yellow. Tools to use are eggs, baskets, and green clothing. Energies involved are birthing, sprouting, and greening. Associated goddesses are Ostara, Kore, and the Maiden. Associated gods are Hare and the Green Man. Appropriate rituals include breakthrough, new growth, new projects, and seed blessings. Common customs include egg games, egg baskets, and wearing new clothing, especially the color green.

Beltane

Also called May Eve, May Day, or Walpurgis Night. Dates covered are around April 30th to early May. Associated colors are the rainbow spectrum, blue, green, pastels and, in fact, all colors! Tools to use are the Maypole and ribbons, flower crowns, fires, bowers, and fields. Energies involved are youthful play, exuberance, sensuality, and pleasure. Associated goddesses are the May Queen and Flora. Associated gods are the May King and Jack-in-the-Green. Appropriate rituals include love, romance, fertility, crop blessings, and creativity endeavours. Common customs include Maypole dancing, mating, flower baskets, and fire jumping.

Midsummer

Also called the Summer Solstice, Litha, or St. John's Day. Dates covered are around June 21st. Associated colors are yellow, gold, and the rainbow colors. Tools to use are bonfires, the Sun wheel, and Earth circles of stone. Energies involved: mainly partnership. Associated goddesses are Mother Earth and Mother Nature. Associated gods: Father Sun/Sky and the Oak King. Appropriate rituals include community, career, relationships, nature

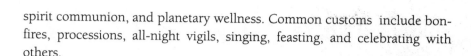

spirit communion, and planetary wellness. Common customs include bonfires, processions, all-night vigils, singing, feasting, and celebrating with
others.

Lammas
Also called Lughnasadh, Lughnasath, or August Eve. Dates covered are
around August 2nd and early August. Associated colors are orange, yellow,
brown, and green. Tools to use are the sacred loaf of bread, harvested herbs,
and bonfires. Energies involved are fruitfulness and reaping prosperity.
Associated goddesses are Demeter, Ceres, and the Corn Mother. Associated
gods are the Grain God, Lugh, and John Barleycorn. Appropriate rituals
include prosperity, generosity, and continued success. Common customs
include games, country fairs, and the offering of first fruits and grains.

Autumn Equinox
Also called Mabon, Michaelmas, or the Fall Equinox. Dates covered are
around September 21st. Associated colors are orange, red, brown, purple,
and blue. Tools to use are cornucopia, corn, and harvested crops. Energies
involved are appreciation and harvest. Associated goddesses are Bona Dea
and the Land Mother. Associated gods are Mabon and the Sky Father.
Appropriate rituals include thanksgiving, harvest, and introspection. Common customs include preparing for the cold weather, bringing in the harvest, and making offerings to the land.

Samhain
Also called Halloween, All Hallows' Eve, All Saints', All Souls', the Feast of
the Dead, or Day of the Dead. Dates covered are October 31st and early
November. Associated colors are black, orange, and indigo. Tools to use are
votive candles, magic mirrors, cauldrons, pumpkins, and divination tools.
Energies involved are death and transformation. It is the Wiccan new year.
The associated goddesses are Crone and Hecate. The associated gods are the
Horned Hunter, Cernunnos, and Anubis. Appropriate rituals include the
honoring of ancestors, releasing the past or dead, foreseeing the future, and
understanding death and rebirth. Common customs include jack-o-
lanterns, spirit plates, the ancestral altar, and divination.

The Eight Pagan Sabbats

SABBAT	DATES	COLORS	ENERGIES	DEITIES
Candlemas, Imbolc, Oimelc, Brigid's Day, Groundhog Day	From around 2nd to 14th February	White, red	Conception, inspiration, initiation	Brigid, the Maiden, the young Sun, the Groundhog
Spring Equinox, Ostara, Easter, Saint Patrick's Day	Around 21st March	Green, yellow	Birthing, sprouting, greening	Ostara, Kore, the Maiden, Hare, the Green Man
Beltane, May Eve, Walpurgis Night, May Day	Around 30th April or 1st May	Rainbow colors	Youthful play, exuberance, sensuality,	May Queen, May King Jack-in-the-Green, Flora
Midsummer, Summer Solstice, Saint John's Day, Litha	Around 21st June	Yellow, gold	Partnership	Mother Earth, Mother Nature, the Oak King, Father Sun
Lammas, August Eve, Lughnasadh, Lughnasath	Around 2nd August (early August)	Orange, yellow, brown, green	Fruitfulness, prosperity	Demeter, Ceres, Lugh, Corn Mother, the Grain God, John Barleycorn

Yule

Also called the Winter Solstice, Jul, Saturnalia, Christmas, or solar/secular New Year. Dates covered are around December 21st. Associated colors are brown, red, green, and white. Tools to use are mistletoe, evergreen wreath, lights, gifts, holly, Yule log, and Yule trees. Energies involved are regeneration and renewal. The associated goddesses are the Great Mother, Isis, Mary, Tonazin, Lucina, and Bona Dea. The associated gods are the Sun Child, Horus, Jesus, Mithras, Santa, Odin, Saturn, and the Holly King. Appropriate rituals include personal renewal, world peace, honoring family and

SABBAT	DATES	COLORS	ENERGIES	DEITIES
Autumn Equinox, *Michaelmas,* *Fall Equinox* *(USA),* *Mabon*	Around 21st September	Orange, red, brown, purple, blue	Appreciation, harvest	Bona Dea, the Land Mother, the Sky Father, Mabon
Samhain, *Halloween,* *All Hallows' Eve,* *All Saints',* *All Souls',* *Feast of the Dead,* *Day of the Dead*	31st October	Black, orange, indigo	Transformation, death	Crone, Hecate, Cernunnos, the Horned Hunter, Anubis
Yule, *Christmas,* *Winter Solstice,* *Jul, Saturnalia,* *Solar New Year*	From around 21st to 31st December	Green, white, brown, red	Regeneration, renewal	Isis, Mary, Lucina, Tonazin, the Great Mother, Bona Dea, Horus, Jesus, the Holly King, Odin, Mithras, Saturn, Saint Nicholas (Santa Claus)

friends. Common customs include wreaths, lights, gift-giving, singing, feasting, and making resolutions.

THE SEASONS OF THE MOON (THE LUNAR MONTH)

Each full cycle of the moon (from the new moon through to the full moon, and back again) takes around 28 days. Depending on its position in the cycle, the moon will have a strong influence on the power and effectiveness of your magickal workings, whether you like it or not.

This isn't because of any arcane awareness, or even necessarily because of the moon's spiritual significance; it's simply because the Earth is affected greatly by the moon's orbit and pull, and your magick draws its power from the Earth's energies. Without a huge reservoir of energy such as the Earth, it would be a lot more difficult to cast effective magick! Consequently, you really need to be very much aware of the moon's influence. And it follows quite logically that you can use the moon's different influences to enhance different types of magick. Working with, rather than against, the moon's energies helps to ensure the best results for your efforts. However, emergencies often arise that can't be postponed until the proper moon cycle. The question then becomes how to work with the current moon's energy to bring about what we need to have happen. The essence of the answer to this question lies in the basics of magick.

Essentially, all magick can be broken down into two types: drawing and banishing. During the waxing moon cycle, your work needs to be concentrated on drawing what you want toward its intended target. During the waning moon, your work needs to be pivoted primarily toward banishing that which you want removed. Therefore, if a sudden illness strikes during the time of the waxing moon, work to draw health rather than banish illness. If an emergency situation calls for a heavy prosperity spell during the time of the waning moon, work toward banishing poverty. As you can see in these situations, the immediate need is accomplished by working with its opposite. In this way, you utilize the energies from the current moon cycle to ultimately achieve your goal.

Of course, none of this is absolutely necessary. By sheer will and personal energy alone, especially if you live in constant awareness of the sacred in everything, you can set events in motion. But, as you've already seen, the moon can really help you. Listed here are the influences of the lunar cycles, along with each of the moon phases, the special moons, and lunar and astrological correspondences.

Waxing cycle moons

This cycle of the moon covers the period from the new moon to the full moon. Its energy should be used in "drawing" what you want toward you. It's a good time to begin new projects and expand any current efforts. It's also a time to craft workings that concern love, harmony, balance, and peace, as well as protection and healing.

New moon
The sun and the moon are in conjunction. The entire moon appears dark.

Waxing crescent moon
There is a light crescent on the right side of the moon.

Waxing half moon
The right half of the moon is lit (90° from the sun — this is the end of the first quarter and the beginning of the second quarter).

Waxing gibbous moon
Three quarters of the moon is now lit.

Full moon
The moon and the sun are in opposition. The entire moon is lit.

Waning cycle moons
The waning cycle of the moon is the period from the full moon to the new moon. This is the cycle to use for banishing and rejecting baneful aspects, such as disease and negativity, as well as dissolving destructive energies of all types.

Full moon
The moon and the sun are in opposition. The entire moon is lit. It's best to wait until three days following the full moon before working with the waning cycle.

Waning crescent moon
There is a dark crescent on the right side of the moon.

Waning half moon
The right half of the moon is now dark (90° from the sun — this is the end of the third quarter and the beginning of the fourth quarter).

Waning gibbous moon
Three quarters of the moon is now dark.

New moon

The sun and the moon are in conjunction. The entire moon appears dark.

Special moons

There are, of course, other lunar energies beyond simple waning and waxing moons. These include each of the phases of the moon within the cycle, as well as special moons, such as the blue moon or an eclipse.

The full moon

The full moon actually covers three days, including the night of the full moon itself. This is a time for action, for harvesting the fruits of our labors, completing things which were begun at the last cycle, and for giving thanks.

The Moon Cycles

WAXING MOON CYCLE

New (Dark) Moon	Waxing Crescent Moon	Waxing Half Moon	Waxing Gibbous Moon	Full (Bright) Moon

WANING MOON CYCLE

Full (Bright) Moon	Waning Crescent Moon	Waning Half Moon	Waning Gibbous Moon	New (Dark) Moon

The dark moon

The dark moon is the three-day period from the last sliver of moonlight to the first sliver of moonlight. This is a good time for introspection — for looking within and meditating on your inner being.

Moon void of course

As the moon orbits the Earth, it passes through the twelve signs of the zodiac. A void-of-course moon is the period during which the moon is not in relation to any planets before entering the next zodiac sign. This period can last as little as a few seconds or it can be longer than a day. Because the moon strongly rules the emotions, you can expect to experience feelings of disconnectedness as well as emotional upsets, mood swings, and general variability. As a rule, I've found that it's best to avoid signing contracts, starting rituals, casting spells, or beginning anything that requires emotional commitment until the moon enters the next sign.

Blue moon

When the full moon turns up twice in one month, it's called a blue moon (also a goal moon). It's a good time to set new (or improved) goals for yourself. Since it takes place so infrequently, you can see why some people describe a rare event as happening "once in a blue moon." Stay alert and watch for them — you'll see only a handful of them in your whole life.

Eclipses

Lunar eclipses represent the perfect union of the sun and moon, so it's fair to say that any kind of magick worked (and any energy sent out) during an eclipse will be amplified tremendously — and the more complete the eclipse, the better. A total eclipse of the sun is one of the most powerful sun-moon events you can hope to use.

THE SEASONS OF THE WEEK (THE DAYS)

In addition to the phases of the moon, there are seven more obvious moon and sun phases in every week: the days of the week. Each day has traditional associations that have been used and proved by magick users across the centuries. Be warned: If the moon is waxing (or is full), then the associations for each day will be in a constructive mode. If the moon is waning (or is dark), then the associations for each day will be in a destructive mode. If you plan to use these week-phases and their associations in your magick, make sure you know which phase the moon is in at the time!

Sunday

Sunday is linked with our star, the sun. It is associated with light, fire, warmth, growth, life, healing, advance and progress, logic, thought, all spiritual matters, and enlightenment.

Monday

Monday relates to the moon, and is a particularly good time for psychic sensitivity and divination skills. As a result, it is perhaps the strongest time of week for intuition. Because of its lunar (moon) influence, it is associated with changing tides, water, and with human emotions and feelings.

Tuesday

Tuesday is linked with the planet Mars. It is associated with action, vigor, assertiveness, violence, courage, vitality, and battles.

Wednesday

Wednesday is linked with the planet Mercury. It is associated with time, action, money, communication, travel, flight, efficiency, speed, and movement in general.

Thursday

Thursday is linked with the planet Jupiter. It is associated with public activity, politics, leadership, wealth, power, strength, anything of huge mass or weight, success, greed, and human charisma.

Friday

Friday is linked with the planet Venus. It is associated with love, marriage, sexual activity, beauty, appearances, attractions, friendship, and also anything visual.

THE DAYS OF THE WEEK

DAY	SYMBOL	GOVERNOR	ASSOCIATIONS
Sunday	☉	The Sun	Light, warmth, fire, growth, healing, progress, logic, thought, enlightenment, spirituality
Monday	☽	The Moon	Psychic ability, divination, intuition, water, changing tides, emotions
Tuesday	♂	Mars	Action, vigor, assertiveness, violence, courage, battles
Wednesday	☿	Mercury	Time, action, money, efficiency, travel, communication, flight, speed, movement
Thursday	♃	Jupiter	Public activity, politics, power, leadership, wealth, strength, huge masses, weight, success, greed, charisma
Friday	♀	Venus	Love, marriage, sexual activity, beauty, anything visual, friendships
Saturday	♄	Saturn	Sickness, health, death, shortage of time, limitations, inactivity, silence, stillness, poverty, authority, knowledge, understanding

Saturday

Saturday is linked with the planet Saturn. It is associated with sickness and health, death, limitation, boundaries, stoppages, shortage of time, inactivity, disability, poverty, silence, stillness, slowness, authority, and also with knowledge and understanding.

MAGICKAL TOOLS AND TALISMANS

Literally hundreds of different tools and talismans are used for multiple purposes in various traditions, rituals, and circumstances. The area of magickal equipment can feel like a bit of a mine field unless you already know what tools are essential. The trick is to own and use only the tools that you need. Don't clutter your cupboard and altar with unnecessary stuff!

As with all things magickal, it is best if there is something of yourself in each tool. If you are able to make your own tools from scratch, that is the ideal situation, but you can buy ready-made tools from most magickal suppliers. If you're feeling extravagant, you could even commission a craftsman to make tools for you. If you choose to buy tools, don't try to knock the price down or bargain for them; if they are the right tools for you, they are invaluable and you need to be grateful that they are available to you at any price! Here listed (in alphabetical order) are the most common tools magick users of all persuasions may want to use.

Athame

The athame (also known as a witches' knife) is most often a black-handled, double-edged knife, although it can take any form that is convenient, provided that it has a clearly defined handle or gripping area, blade, or stem area, and a point or tip. Natural magick users often opt for a hand-hewn athame cut from a tree or branch, often burned and polished to make it jet black.

Aspergillis (Asperger)

The aspergillis (also known as an asperger) is a device for sprinkling liquids such as water or wine in ritual. It is traditionally made of sprigs of mint, rosemary, and marjoram (or a similar herb) tied together with red silk. If that is not an option, any other method will suffice — why not use a small sponge attached to the end of a wooden handle?

Bell (Gong)

A bell or gong can be used to awaken the elements in the earlier stages of ritual. This is not currently a very common practice.

Bolline

Traditionally a white-handled knife, the bolline is used for carving, inscribing, and cutting during ritual. Talismans may be inscribed or carved; candles may be cut or inscribed; ropes or cords may be cut. A single-edged blade is sufficient.

Book of Shadows (and Enchantments)

The Book of Shadows (also called the Book of Shadows and Enchantments) is a personally kept journal of spells, rituals, recipes, divinations, and other magickal details. Some initiates choose to write in code or in runes for secrecy and safety (although that makes it very difficult to read by flickering candlelight, as is so often necessary!).

Candles

Wax candles (preferably natural beeswax) are used frequently for a number of purposes, including ritual symbols, candle magick (a whole subject in its own right), or just plain old atmospheric lighting. They often have inscriptions, runes, or other symbology carved on them.

Cauldron

The cauldron is a pot into which the physical components or ingredients of a ritual may be thrown. It does not necessarily have to be used for "cooking" or boiling ingredients, although that is a good way of creating herbal potions and compounds.

Chalice

The chalice is a cup or goblet that is used for sharing wine among those present in a magick circle. It is associated specifically with the water element and with the Goddess.

Cords (Ropes)

Cords can be used in the binding and releasing of magick, as a symbol of a physical binding or releasing, or as a girdle about a magick user's waist (in which case its color often indicates the wearer's degree of initiation or magickal achievement).

Lamps of Art

The lamps of art are simply two or more candles that are placed on an altar to provide illumination during a ritual. The colors of the candles are often chosen to coincide with seasonal influences (either magickal seasons or the actual seasons of the year).

Mirror (Dark Mirror, Magick Mirror)

The magick mirror or dark mirror acts as a portal or window to other realms, planes, and dimensions. It also functions as a means of communication with other spiritual entities, a means for divination (scrying), and even as a store or shield for psychic energies. Dark mirrors are specially shaped (they're round, slightly concave, and highly polished) out of blackened glass to provide a focus for your attention, so that you're not distracted by anything else that's going on around you. Despite its name, it isn't really a mirror at all! Dark mirrors can be any size from a few inches to a few feet across and are best constructed from slightly concave glass, blackened on one side. In a pinch, for scrying, you could try using a regular mirror covered with black, non-reflective cloth or paper — but it isn't likely to be quite as helpful to you as a true dark mirror would be.

Pen of Art

This is a pen reserved exclusively for writing in your Book of Shadows and Enchantments. Sometimes a quill pen and ink are used, although this can become quite cumbersome if you need to write quickly.

Pentagram (Pentacle)

This is the mystic and magickal symbol of the five-pointed star, generally made out of a flat disc of metal, wood, or ceramic. It can be used in ritual as a symbol of balance, as a magickal shield, or as a representation of wholeness (for example, representing the whole planet Earth).

Salt Bowl

A small open container, the salt bowl is reserved exclusively for holding salt for ritual use. A common design is a shallow, polished metal dish with a pentagram engraved on the surface.

Staff

The staff is a highly personal tool, usually hewn from a large tree branch and carved or fashioned by hand. The staff acts as an enormous reservoir of aetheric energy and pre-enchanted magickal power, able to release its charge at the sorcerer's command. Every sorcerer should have a solid, dependable staff of his or her own. It is not a walking stick, by the way — it is more like the magickal equivalent of a portable electric generator!

Statues

Statues of the Goddess and the God are placed on the altar as symbols of their presence. The Goddess is represented as a beautiful, skyclad woman, the God as a powerful, vital, skyclad, horned man. The statues have been used less and less frequently in recent times.

Stones (Crystals)

Crystals often appear on ritual altars because they have some unique properties, such as being able to collect or filter aetheric energy. Some enchantments may be "stored" in crystals while they are working (thus forming a crystal charm, amulet, or talisman).

Sword

A sword is sometimes used to define, or cast, the perimeter of the magick circle in ritual. It is normally associated with the elements of fire and air.

Thurible

The thurible is a brazier for ritual incense. It is generally metal, with a chain or handle for use when it is hot. Inside the thurible you would place a layer of sand and some glowing embers or burning charcoal. You would add a few pinches of incense when needed.

Wand

The wand is generally a wooden stick as long as the distance from your elbow to your fingertips. Usually carved from a sacred wood, it is used to channel energy (although that is just as easily achieved using an athame) and to accumulate energy for short periods of time. Often the wand will have a crystal embedded at one end to act as a point of focus.

Water Bowl

This is a small, open container reserved exclusively for holding purified water for ritual use. A common design is a shallow, polished metal dish with a pentagram engraved on the surface. A small jug is also frequently used.

BLESSING THE TOOLS...

The blessing or enchanting of your magickal equipment is entirely optional, but it will help to keep your tools in harmony with your magickal workings, so it's well worth the time and effort involved. You may name your tools, if you wish. You need to give each tool or talisman a very specific lifetime, whether that's a matter of minutes, hours, days, weeks, months, or years. A very common and, in my opinion, brilliant idea is to specifically grant each tool your own lifetime. That way your tools will die with you, and nobody will be able to take advantage of your aetheric energies after you've gone! Tools that are generally worth blessing (consecrating) or enchanting with power include athames, bowls, cups, pentacles, staffs, statues, swords, wands, and any other symbols or jewelry that you use regularly.

In addition to the usual tools of magick, there is the talisman (also known as an amulet or charm). This is normally a stone or an item of wearable jewelry carrying a protective inscription or carving somewhere on it or in it. By the way, the word "talisman" comes from the Medieval Greek *telesma,* meaning "ritual," and "amulet" is from the Latin *amuletum,* which is "a protection from evil." A talisman is usually designed to protect its wearer from evil forces and influences. There are a number of popular folk myths concerning natural talismans, such as the crucifix or garlic to ward off vampires, silver bullets against the werewolf, and so forth, but whether they are as effective as folk legend suggests remains to be seen (unless you have firsthand experience, in which case I'd love to hear from you via the publishers!). Creating a talisman or amulet is a very simple matter: select the stone or jewelry that you want to use and then enchant it with any spell of protection, no matter how simple. Remember to give the talisman a life span that fits its purpose. That's all there is to it. Just one final warning: It is best not to sell protection (or profit from it), as that may cause the Goddess and the God to reconsider the terms under which they will protect you while you're working in the aethereal realm. Even for simple charms and amulets, your motives are still the most important factor in the success of your magick.

PROTECT AND SURVIVE

Now that leads us to something else that's worth considering: When you're casting magick, accessing the aethereal realm, channeling, or even just working with vibrational energies, you're also likely to be putting yourself in a situation where other spiritual forces can find you — or worse still, be attracted to you by your use of aethereal energy. In most cases, this is likely to be pretty harmless and you probably won't often be doing anything that makes a big enough splash to attract unwanted attention. The problem arises when you're raising or using a large amount of energy, or even a small amount of any particularly pure energy. That special energy may inadvertently attract other beings. At times such as these, you may be in danger — spiritually, physically, or both! Protection is something that you shouldn't be without when you're casting magick. Obviously, some Envisioned and Low magick won't be a problem, but even so it's a good idea to consider the energies involved before you cast any magick on any occasion. If you decide that you want to protect yourself and reduce the chances of your magick being interfered with, there are several ways of doing so.

The Magick Circle is perhaps the most common system of magickal protection for ritual and magick work. When you cast (create) a Magick Circle, you are setting up a physical and aethereal boundary around the sacred space in which you plan to work your magick and ritual. This sacred space protects those within it from outside influences and distractions. It also serves to contain and concentrate energy that is raised until you deliberately release or channel it. The biggest problem you face when using a Magick Circle is that you must never break the circle's boundary, either by touching the aethereal curtain that surrounds it or by breaking, disturbing, or crossing the physical boundary. If you do, the circle will collapse around you and can leave you subject to untold aetheric energy surges and rifts — a situation that leads to energy imbalances in your body and very often even physical ailments, such as disorientation, headaches, nausea, weakness, tiredness, and similar complaints. If this should happen, immediately ground yourself to rebalance your body's elemental energies. This is easily achieved either by visualization or by physically touching something of nature that is in contact with the earth (such as the ground, a tree, a stream, etc.).

The Protective Amulet is often put to work by magick users when, due to their circumstances, surroundings, or situation, they are not able to create a Magick Circle. For example, it is difficult to cast a circle in a very confined space, or in complete darkness, on uneven terrain, in somebody else's house, or where there is a risk of being disturbed, or — the list is endless.

The Protective Spell (also known as a Protective Enchantment) is often employed by magick users when they have no other means of quickly protecting themselves, such as a Protective Amulet, and are not able to create a Magick Circle due to circumstances. It is worth keeping in mind that the spell, if cast by the person whom it protects, is only effective as long as they keep their concentration; in other words, if anything happens to make their concentration lapse, the Protective Spell may stop working! For this reason it is often wiser to find a fellow magick user who will cast the Protective Spell for them to make sure that it doesn't falter while they are working.

The Protected Place is rare, a place in which no outside forces or energies can reach you. It is an aethereally isolated space, the only entrance to which is in the physical world. If you find such a place, you need to test it thoroughly to make sure it doesn't leak aetheric energy. As a simple test, send out psychic "waves" of energy, and try to sense how soon the waves lose their power. A short time — perhaps a few minutes or less — would suggest that the place isn't very "energy-tight."

Once you are sure of its security, you will be able to use that place instead of casting a Magick Circle, carrying a Protective Amulet, or casting Protective Spells. If you want to find such a place, the most obvious ones are naturally formed granite caves that have only one narrow entrance, which you would consecrate with salt when you are inside. Despite their rarity, these Protective Places may well be the inspiration for the "wizard's cave" often found in children's stories and fairy tales.

MAKING A MAGICK CIRCLE

The casting of a Magick Circle is a simple ritual involving a few very simple steps: defining the circle's boundary with a curtain of energy, reinforcing the circle against unwanted or evil influences, summoning the Elements to assist in your work, blessing it with consecrated salt and water, and finally protecting (consecrating) the circle's boundary. Try to work in harmony with any appropriate moon phases, if at all possible. Ideally, your rituals and spells should be worked outside, as close to nature as possible, preferably at night. Try to work where you can be in silence, undiscovered, and uninterrupted.

Before starting to cast a circle, you need to make sure you have everything you need. Here are a few simple guidelines for preparation:

❖ Remove, hide, or cover all timekeepers (clocks, watches, etc.).

❖ Remove all unnecessary clothing within reason, comfort, and prudence.

❖ Darken, as much as possible, the space in which you will work, while still allowing yourself sufficient light to be able to read your scripts.

For this very simple solitary Magick Circle casting shadow, you will need these items:

❖ an athame

❖ a white candle (with an appropriate stand or support)

❖ a glass containing water (spring water or distilled water, if available)

❖ a glass containing a thin layer of salt (sea-salt or unrefined salt, if possible)

❖ a dark mirror (or, in a pinch, a silver one covered with nonreflective black cloth or paper)

❖ a rope of at least 260 inches (about 6.5m) in length.

The rope is there only to define the physical boundary of the circle; if you have some other method of defining the circle's boundary (such as chalk or scoring a line on the ground), you could do that instead.

Making the circle

Find approximate North using the stars, a compass, or any other means available. Take up the long rope and form it into a circle on the ground around you, both starting and ending at the East — overlapping the ends slightly — to form a closed circle. You may leave or enter the circle freely (by stepping over the boundary rope) until the casting is completed, but do not break the circle (by separating the ends of the rope).

Place the glasses of water and of salt, the mirror, the candle, and your athame inside the circle to the North side. Light the candle and leave it burning undisturbed for the duration of the session. Bring into the circle any other tools or equipment that will be needed later, because you won't be able to get out to fetch them after the circle is cast!

Stand in the middle of the circle and, beginning at the East, use your athame to trace the edge of the circle sunwise (clockwise in the northern hemisphere), envisioning an aetheric curtain of power springing up as you go (this is often envisioned as white or purple light). Trace the circle three times, ending up with the curtain of aetheric light fully surrounding you. While tracing the circle three times, utter:

> *Closed may this circle be,*
> *Under the protection of the Goddess.*
> *Protect and guide me, O Gracious One,*
> *For all that is within*
> *Shall be between the worlds*
> *Until it be broken.*

Now put down the athame and pick up the mirror. Hold it facing you, pointing toward it with the first two fingers of your right hand, and utter:

> *Now do I breathe in, and out, deeply.*
> *But it is not merely air that I take in —*
> *It is the white, clear light which pervades the universe.*
> *I breathe in with my entire body, not just my lungs*
> *And I breathe out pure light and life force into this mirror,*
> *From whence its good powers will light up this circle,*
> *So that no evil may enter.*
> *So mote it be.*

Place the mirror faceup on the ground at the North of the circle. Take up your athame and point it toward the East, uttering:

> *Thou spirits of Air,*
> *I do bid thee come*

> *To be about me in this circle*
> *That I may know thee better.*
> *Blessed be!*

Facing next to the South, utter:

> *Thou spirits of Fire,*
> *I do bid thee come*
> *To be about me in this circle*
> *That I may know thee better.*
> *Blessed be!*

Facing next to the West, utter:

> *Thou spirits of Water,*
> *I do bid thee come*
> *To be about me in this circle*
> *That I may know thee better.*
> *Blessed be!*

Facing finally to the North, utter:

> *Thou spirits of Earth,*
> *I do bid thee come*
> *To be about me in this circle*
> *That I may know thee better.*
> *Blessed be!*

Lay down the athame and take up the glass of salt in your left hand. Point the first two fingers of your right hand at the salt, uttering:

> *I exorcise thee, creature of Earth,*
> *By the gracious, lovely, and powerful Goddess*
(here make the sign of the pentagram above the glass)
> *That thou may be purified of all evil influences,*
> *In Her name.*

(here extend your flattened palm over the glass)
> *Creature of Earth, adore thy Creatrix.*
> *In the Name of our gracious Lady I consecrate thee*

(here make the sign of the pentagram above the glass)
> *To the service of the Lady, and Her Craft.*
> *So mote it be.*

Set down the glass of salt and take up the glass containing the water, and utter:

> *I exorcise thee, creature of Water,*
> *By the gracious, lovely, and powerful Goddess*

(here make the sign of the pentagram above the glass)
> *That thou may be purified of all evil influences,*
> *In Her name.*

(here extend your flattened palm over the glass)
> *Creature of Water, adore thy Creatrix.*
> *In the Name of our gracious Lady I consecrate thee*

(here make the sign of the pentagram above the glass)
> *To the service of the Lady, and Her Craft.*
> *So mote it be.*

Pick up the salt and cast it into the water, then set down the empty salt glass. Hold the glass of salt and water in both hands, uttering:

> *I pray thee, my Goddess of things wild and free,*
> *That thou may stretch forth thy right hand of power*
> *Upon these creatures of the elements,*
> *And hallow them in thy Holy Name.*
> *Grant that this salt may make for health of body*
> *And this water for health of soul,*
> *And that there may be banished*
> *From the place where they are used,*
> *Every power of adversity, and every illusion,*
> *And every artifice of evil.*
> *In thy Holy Name, so mote it be.*

Starting at the East and working sunwise as before, lightly sprinkle the boundary of the circle (taking care not to disturb or break the circle). The circle is cast. Now you can safely get on with any rituals and spells that you want to work.

BREAKING A MAGICK CIRCLE

It is extremely important that you break (dissolve) your Magick Circle properly after you have finished your work. If you don't break it in a correct and ordered way, you would, in effect, be causing a rupture in the circle when you leave it — which would open you up to all the same dangers associated with breaking the circle accidentally.

The procedure outlined here is very simple. It's almost an exact reverse of the procedure outlined for casting the circle in the first place. You start by thanking the Elemental forces for being with you and helping you. Then you draw back the circle's curtain of aetheric power into the mirror for safekeeping, and finally you break the physical boundary. It is also a good idea to eat a meal afterwards, because that has the effect of grounding your body's elemental energies and starting the process of rebalancing your aetheric energy.

Breaking the circle
Stand in the middle of the circle, facing East. Take up your athame and point it toward the East, uttering:

> *Thou spirits of Air,*
> *I thank thee for being near.*
> *I bid you a cordial farewell.*
> *Blessed be!*

Facing next to the South, utter:

> *Thou spirits of Fire,*
> *I thank thee for being near.*
> *I bid you a cordial farewell.*
> *Blessed be!*

Facing next to the West, utter:

> *Thou spirits of Water,*
> *I thank thee for being near.*
> *I bid you a cordial farewell.*
> *Blessed be!*

Facing next to the North, utter:

> *Thou spirits of Earth,*
> *I thank thee for being near.*
> *I bid you a cordial farewell.*
> *Blessed be!*

Now lay down the athame and take up the mirror so that it faces straight upwards, and utter:

> *This time is ended,*
> *The spirits depart to their strange lands.*
> *The powers about this circle*
> *are drawn into the mirror.*
> *There they remain*
> *Until summoned again.*
> *So mote it be.*

Lay the mirror facedown on the ground and take up your athame. Use it to break the circle at the East where it began. Extinguish the candle, and utter:

> *The circle is broken.*

Collect your tools, pack them away neatly, and don't forget to tidy up after yourself. After any ritual, it's advisable to balance and ground yourself (allowing your physical body and aethereal body to reharmonize themselves). This process will help your body to expel any unneeded energies that have built up (or been absorbed) during the ritual, and to regain energy that has been spent in creating the magick. For countless centuries, a hearty meal after the ritual has provided not only a physical grounding influence but also a great social occasion for the celebration of our successes and beliefs.

CHAPTER 4

SHADOW MAGICK

WHAT'S IN A RITUAL?

S mall Shadow magick is ritual magick that has mainly natural effects, in accordance with the commonly accepted laws of both nature and physics, while Arcane Shadow Magick is ritual magick that operates mainly outside of those laws. For many traditions of witchcraft, Small Shadow magick is the first that is witnessed by a new or potential initiate at a coven meeting. It is, essentially, practical natural magick that is formed powerfully by several magick users working together in the ritual.

In both Small and Arcane Shadow magick, there is often some degree of drama (or even melodrama) to illustrate the purpose of the ritual, and to focus the minds of everyone taking part.

When you're thinking about planning a ritual or a spell, it is vitally important to understand exactly what goes into making magick — the very source of sorcery. Imagine, if you will, the pure and precise ringing sound that you hear from a well-made church bell. Now think about how the traditional church bell is made. It is essentially a huge lump of metal, so it can't easily be shaped out of a block of metal, nor can it be constructed out of lots of smaller metal bits. It would be impractical to manufacture, and it certainly wouldn't have the clear metallic ringing sound of a single-piece cast bell. No, the bell has to be cast by pouring molten metal into a bell mold, and leaving it to cool and set before mounting it in the church tower and striking it with a hammer to make that pure sound.

Look at magick in the same way. Think of the effect of your magick as being the ringing sound that the bell makes: it's the part that everybody can witness for themselves. It's the result of two things: the bell being made properly in the correct shape, and the bell being struck with the hammer. If either one of those qualities is missing, the bell doesn't ring! So the ring is the magickal effect or the result.

The bell itself is the Spell that shapes the energy provided by the hammer. If the bell is warped into the wrong shape, all you would hear is a dull thud as the hammer strikes. It is the shape that determines what noise the bell will make, and in magickal terms it is the Spell that determines the result.

But all that is irrelevant until somebody puts some energy into the shape. You can make a perfect bell out of the best metal and smooth its sides to perfection, but that bell will never make a noise if nobody strikes it. The act of empowering a Spell is the same as striking the bell: it fills the shape with energy and causes the effect to actually take place.

The hammer is simply the method by which you empower the Spell. In this case, you are using a ritual to create the shape and punch the power into it. If you were casting a Spell without using a ritual then you would have to create the shape of the Spell by some other means (for example, using words, thoughts, or symbology), and you would have to find a way of empowering it.

PREPARING A NEW RITUAL

This section will guide you through the preparation of a new ritual. It's a very exciting thing to do, because you're starting with nothing and ending up with a new spell that's going to make a difference to somebody! There are several things that need to be considered carefully before you can create a new ritual that is going to work effectively and safely:

❖ The intention of the ritual
❖ The equipment and ingredients needed
❖ Any physical preparations needed
❖ Any magickal preparations needed
❖ The actual ritual script and procedure
❖ Any final actions to carry out afterwards

The intention...

Most successful ideas in life seem to begin with a problem that needs a solution. You will probably find the same thing when you want to create a ritual. There will be a problem or a situation that you believe will be best resolved or affected by magick. The intention of the ritual is a description of what should be achieved by the successful and honest casting of the spell. As we work through this section, we will follow the construction of a simple ritual for banishing unwanted emotions from your life. The intention section might look like this:

To banish a problem from your mind and from your life.

Now you need to consider any ethical or moral implications. It's all very well to create a ritual for your specific short-term needs, but remember that once it has been written down, it will probably be used again in the future.

First of all, you need to examine the intention in the light of both the Sorcerer's Code and the Wiccan Rede. If it does not live up to those ideals, I would suggest you rethink your motives.

Next, you need to ask yourself two simple questions about it. If your answer is "yes" to either question, don't continue:

❖ Would I mind if somebody else cast this magick?
❖ Would I mind being affected by this magick?

As a final safety check, think carefully about the possible consequences of the magick you are planning. At all times, keep in mind the Law of Cause and Effect (also known as the karma principle or the law of return). If you use magick to change something here and now, somewhere later on there will be an equal reaction (or worse, you might cause an avalanche effect and end up with a chain reaction coming back at you). Likewise, whatever you change now may cause an unforeseen chain reaction of its own! You know that when you topple the first domino, the rest of the line will fall over. But if you couldn't see the rest of the line behind the first domino, you wouldn't know that you were about to topple them all, would you? The best you can do is to look as hard as you can for other consequences that might arise and avoid doing anything that would cause uncontrolled reactions like that unseen domino line. Remember that even the simple act of banishing a problem from your life might cause some kind of karmic backlash later on! The importance of wise consideration of the use of magick can't be overemphasized.

Equipment and ingredients

When you write up your ritual script, you need to tell the readers very clearly what they need to gather together for the whole ritual, from start to finish. Most often that will include anything they need for before, during, and after the ritual. There's nothing more aggravating when performing a ceremony than realizing you didn't bring the matches to light the ritual candles!

Ritual ingredients are generally the first things listed. These are the items that are specific to a particular ritual. Examples of these include candles of various colors and composition, incense, herbs, oils, plant extracts and leaves, stones, hair or feathers, photographs or symbols, different types of wood, natural cloths, threads, or cords, various minerals, and even vegetables. Almost anything can be used as a ritual ingredient. You need to decide on a list of ingredients based on past experience, accepted wisdom, and common symbology. Use what you know works, what others have used effectively in the past, and what others accept as representing the things you want to achieve. Use to your advantage the accepted mystical significances of timing, distances and sizes, colors, shapes, materials, textures, smells, sounds, and even taste (there are many hundreds of good books on the subject that are generally in agreement). The most important thing is to be sure of the reasons for using each of the ingredients in your ritual, and what magickal purpose each ingredient serves; otherwise you won't fully understand the shape of the spell that will be created by the ritual.

Ritual tools are often listed immediately after the ingredients. These are the magickal tools or equipment needed during the ritual. Examples of these include the athame (black knife), aspergillis, bell, bolline (white knife), altar candles, cauldron, ropes, dark mirror, pentagram shield, staff, statues, sword, thurible (incense burner), wand, salt bowl, and water bowl.

Finally you'll need to list any other practical aids that will be needed. These are things that aren't specifically involved with the ritual but are necessary anyway. These include items such as matches, candleholders, wrapping cloths, bags, boxes, and wire or string (for tying ingredients together). When your ritual is basically complete, walk through it in your mind and make sure that everything you would use is somewhere on the equipment list.

In the case of our example, "Banishing a Problem," the ritual is so simple and basic that it doesn't need any magickal protection — such as a magick circle — so there's no need to list any tools or ingredients that would be needed for that. For the equipment list, however, we need a large, healthy apple, which will be cut up during the ritual. It seems obvious, then, that a sharp knife will also be required. The final equipment and ingredients list will look something like this:

❖ The largest apple you can find

❖ A sharp knife (for cutting up the apple)

Physical preparations...

The physical preparations section is where you provide instruction on the best places, surroundings, and conditions in which to perform the ritual. Some rituals need to be performed outdoors (particularly those working directly with nature, the Earth, the moon, the sun, or any of the planets). Others need to be performed in the place where they are to take effect (such as exorcisms and blessings).

Regardless of the physical preparations, it is always worth putting in a note about any mental preparations that would make the ritual easier. For example, if there is a lot of mental imagery or psychic transference in the ritual itself, it's a good idea to include a note in this section to tell readers to relax and calm their minds first. I usually include the text of the Divine Prayer, which is a great help in relaxing both mind and body. You'll find The Divine Prayer on page 1 of this book.

While you're considering the physical preparations, it's important to make sure that your instructions can be realistically carried out without needing a geographically specific location. In other words, you won't be able to create a ritual of global use if you need to be standing at the bottom of the Grand Canyon when you perform it.

Other things to consider in preparing your ritual are practicalities such as darkness and illumination (darkness provides atmosphere but means that you can't read the script easily). Consider clothing or otherwise (skyclad ritual gets you close to nature, but isn't a good idea if it's very cold). Consider preparing food and drink for when the performance of the ritual is finished.

Magickal preparations...

The magickal preparations section is where you need to instruct the reader on the best magickal circumstances for the ritual. Some rituals need to be planned to coincide with specific moon phases, days of the week, or special seasons of the year, so here you would provide details of which times and seasons are best.

Magickal protection is something that, ideally, you should not have to remind the reader about, but it's so important that it's worth mentioning every time. Of course, some rituals don't need any specific magickal protection, because they don't directly manipulate or open energy channels to other realms and dimensions. As a rough guide, you need to work within a magickally protected area if:

❖ The ritual involves establishing contact with aethereal, elemental, or Divine entities.

❖ The ritual involves channeling aethereal or elemental energies from one plane to another.

❖ The ritual involves manipulating aethereal or elemental energies outside of your own body, which includes trapping, releasing, shaping, amplifying, or modifying those energies.

❖ The ritual involves manipulation of your aethereal body, including astral travel, out-of-body experiences, and spiritual healing.

There's no need to include the complete magick circle-casting ritual in this section, because that's a basic ritual that all magick users should already have in their own Book of Shadows. All you have to do is make it very clear that magickal protection is needed — and list the necessary items in your equipment and ingredients list. I normally list the ingredients and equipment for the magick circle separately from the other items, so that the reader can see which items aren't specifically involved with the ritual itself — in case they have some alternative method of protection that they would like to use, or an alternative ritual for casting the magick circle.

Our example, "Banishing a Problem," doesn't touch on any of the usual danger areas, so there's no need to include any notes on protection. Likewise, it isn't specifically aimed at any season, moon phase, or day of the week, so there are no magickal preparation notes to make.

The ritual script and procedure...

The ritual script is what you've been building up to with your equipment and preparations. Not surprisingly, you'll need to have a fairly good idea of what's in this section before you can plan any of the previous sections. In fact, you will find, as you create more and more of your own rituals, that you end up creating all the sections together in a bit-by-bit fashion. As you change something in the script, you need to check that you haven't altered the needs of the other sections, and so on.

This is the section where you effectively organize a stage plan for the whole ritual, from start to finish. You need to make provision for all the possibilities and circumstances that may arise, trying to make the ritual as adaptable as possible. For this reason, you may want to provide alternative texts or procedures for different circumstances. For example, a solitary magick user would say, "I summon thee, element of Air," while a group would collectively say, "We summon thee, element of Air." It is up to you how much you try to cater to all circumstances, but it is worth remembering that the script is probably going to be read at a distance in dim, flickering candlelight, so you might want to keep the word count down as much as possible!

The ritual script needs to include instructions on where each participant should be at any given time, which direction they should be facing, what they should be doing and saying. It is also important to include timing cues for group situations, and explanatory notes if anything is unclear or ambiguous. Also, avoid the "jargon trap." Try not to use long words when short words will do. The last thing any Book of Shadows needs is having to include a glossary of terms!

Something else to consider in constructing a ritual is the balance between words, thoughts, and actions. If the ritual is for a solitary magick user, the balance doesn't matter that much, but in group situations, too much visualizing and not enough words can allow the harmony of minds to be lost. When two or more people are involved, you need verbal or physical cues to coordinate the various visualization and psychic activities.

In the case of our example, "Banishing a Problem," the ritual script is very short and to the point. At this stage, I might include only the information necessary for the performance of the ritual itself, and then, later on, I could perhaps add some other helpful comments and narrative. So far, the ritual script looks something like this:

Focus and concentrate your mind on the apple, then say aloud:

Apple pure, fruit of tree,
Take ye now this ache from me...

Now tell the apple the nature of your problem.

Take the knife and cut the apple into at least four pieces (more, if the problem is very intense).

Go outside and bury the pieces of apple together in the ground. As the apple rots, so will the unwanted problem.

Final actions...

The final actions section serves two purposes. There are sometimes things that need to be done after the ritual is performed, such as disposing of used ingredients, wrapping magickal tools, and tidying up the area. It is important to make sure that you dispose of used ingredients safely and leave your ritual area as it was before you started.

There are also things that need to be either given or told to the subject (the person for whom the magick is being worked). Often the ritual will involve magickally charging an object that you want to give to the subject along with appropriate instructions and warnings. Be very specific in the wording of your instructions and warnings so that there can be no doubt as to their meaning.

In the case of our example, "Banishing a Problem," the final actions section needs to contain only one warning — not to go back and dig up the past again. It may look something like this:

Don't ever dig up the apple again, even if it's only to see if the apple has rotted away yet. The whole point is that you've buried the problem and walked away.

Once you've completed all the sections, go back and make sure that the equipment and ingredients list is still complete and accurate. Then check that the physical and magickal preparations sections still cover everything that they need to, and that they don't contain any unnecessary preparations. Also act out the ritual script step-by-step in your mind (taking care not to actually cast the spell this time!). Make sure that the ritual is physically practical and doesn't require the skills of a contortionist to pick up too many tools or ingredients at once. As a final courtesy to future users of the ritual, check your spelling, punctuation, and grammar to see that there are no ambiguities that could lead to confusion.

COMPLETING THE RITUAL

The preparations for performing an existing ritual are generally simple, because everything tends to revolve around nature (and nature offers a plentiful supply of everything you need). By the way, when you are collecting ritual ingredients, you are expected to act responsibly, keeping in mind at all times the witches' rule: "An ye harm none, do what ye will." Be sure to avoid causing damage to nature, the Earth, or any of her animals!

Your preparations for any kind of ritual will include a lot more than gathering ingredients together. There's the very serious business of enacting, speaking, dancing, or even singing a ritual to create the shape of the magick, along with the act of empowering that shape with whatever combinations of aether, fire, air, water, and earth are needed.

Arguably, the most important factor when setting out to cast any kind of magick is the state of your mind at the time. Regardless of whether the magick being cast is high, low, small, arcane, shadow, enchantment, white or black, you need a calm, controlled, and purposeful mind. In other words, clear your mind of the worries of the day. Past experience shows that concentrating on something intensely helps to center and focus the mind.

It is best to try to relax yourself bodily as well, because a restless body leads inevitably to a restless mind. Once again, experience illuminates the quickest and easiest way to relax fully. Make sure you have plenty of time and that you aren't going to be interrupted. Silence the telephone, close the curtains, turn off the lights (if you want), lie down somewhere comfortable and not too cold, and then begin to relax your body. If you want to close your eyes, feel free to do so, but be aware that you are more likely to fall asleep if you do! Think about relaxing each and every set of muscles, starting at your toes and working up through your whole body. Make a conscious effort to relax as completely as possible. When you are calm and relaxed, don't stand up too quickly. If you do, it can make you feel dizzy, and we don't want you to fall over!

I tend to write up my rituals in a common format (see Chapter Eight — "Grimoire of Shadow Magick") so that others will know roughly what to expect when they're trying to read them in the half-light that so often surrounds a ritual. When you write up your own rituals, fill out the text as much as is necessary to avoid confusion. It's also worth writing the script as if you are talking to the reader, not to yourself. For example, under Equipment Needed, rather than write "a large apple," I wrote "the largest apple you can find." When you are scripting a ritual that others will use, try to think of the reader as a stranger you've never met — you can't assume they know everything that you do.

It's also a very good idea to put in comments about things in the ritual that others may later wonder about. For example, in the Ritual Instructions section for our example ritual, you might want to explain that it is a simple "bind and dispel rite" — if you think the reader might better understand the ritual by knowing that. I would also find a way to make it obvious which words are narrative and which are to be spoken out. With a computer, you can easily use a different typeface or type style. If you're writing the script by hand, perhaps use different color inks, being careful to use colors that can be seen clearly even in dim lighting. As you can see, it's very important to express yourself as fully as possible when you're writing your ritual scripts. The finished "Banishing a Problem" ritual can be found in the Grimoire of Shadow Magick in Chapter Eight.

CHAPTER 5

ENCHANTMENT MAGICK

WHAT'S IN A SPELL?

A spell (an enchantment) is a magickal shape — as you will have found out in earlier chapters — which determines what will happen when that shape is invoked and empowered. In the previous chapter, "Shadow Magick," I likened the making of magick to the making of a church bell. If you haven't read that chapter then you need to go back and read it through carefully now. Returning to the analogy of the church bell, the spell relates to the shape of the bell, which determines the harmonic resonances and sounds that come out of it when raw energy is applied (with a hammer, in the case of a bell). The end result of a successfully performed ritual is a fully empowered spell. Most often, a spell is made into a ritual for one of the following reasons:

❖ The spell would be dangerous if it were cast outside of a magickally protected environment.

❖ The spell needs more power than one person can normally provide.

❖ The spell would involve establishing contact with aethereal, elemental, or Divine entities.

❖ The spell would involve channeling aethereal or elemental energies from one plane to another.

❖ The spell would involve manipulating aethereal or elemental energies outside your own body, including trapping, releasing, shaping, amplifying, or modifying those energies.

❖ The spell would involve manipulation of your aethereal body, including astral travel, out-of-body experiences, and spiritual healing.

Spells have certain obvious advantages over rituals. By far the greatest advantage is that a spell, once learned, can normally be performed on the spur of the moment without any particular preparations, equipment, or ingredients. Coupled with that comes the disadvantage that you seldom have time to think through the consequences of the spell, or have the luxury of planning the timing of the spell to coincide with specific seasons, moon phases, or days of the week.

Another advantage of the spell over the ritual is that it is generally uncomplicated, quick, and discreet to perform, making it useful in almost any circumstance. The disadvantage that goes along with that is that an uncomplicated spell leaves more work to the psychic abilities of the magick user, whereas a ritual can involve more detailed and intimate wording, drama, and symbology. Rituals tend to be well planned and prepared, and their shapes are immaculately detailed. Spells tend to be impromptu, unplanned, and their shapes are left very much to the caster's imagination and past experience.

Another major distinction between the spell and the ritual is the amounts and types of energy that can get involved in the magickal workings. In ritual several people can work together to raise and channel huge amounts of aethereal and elemental energy and direct them using magick tools (such as athames, wands, cords, dark mirrors, and so forth). In a spell you are the only source, conductor, and director of those energies, meaning that it all has to be supplied out of your body's own energies, which you then replenish by grounding yourself afterwards.

When you cast a spell without using a ritual, the spell's shape is formed by your mind alone. If you have previously cast the spell successfully, your mind will already know the shape, and gradually you'll become more proficient at casting it; otherwise, you need to have a very strong and well-trained mind. Powerful psychic abilities are needed in order to even begin to shape a spell accurately in your mind. All spells need concentration and strong self-will, except for the most basic blessings and "wish spells" (those that express a desire and are similar in structure to a simple prayer). If you have not yet developed your psychic visualization and transference abilities to the point of perfection, you need to practice those things before you can be successful in the unaided casting of a spell! In the casting of spells, the old adage "Practice makes perfect" is more true than ever.

PREPARING A NEW SPELL

Creating a new spell is an exciting thing to do, because you're creating something that will make a big difference in somebody's life. By the time you come to create a new spell, you will have already encountered some problem or situation that needs to be resolved or addressed. You have obviously already decided that the best way to tackle it will be by using magick. Now if you want to create a spell, that means you've decided that no magickal protection is required, and that you don't see any need for magick tools or any particular ingredients. If that isn't the case, you should probably be thinking about creating a ritual, not a spell.

A number of things need to be considered carefully before you create a new spell that will be both safe and effective:

❖ Carefully consider the intention of the spell.
❖ Think through any physical and magickal preparations that need to be made first.
❖ Plan the actual enchantment script (or instructions).
❖ Work out the details of any final actions that need to be carried out afterwards (either by you or by the spell's recipient) in order for the spell to work.

You'll notice, as you read on, that much of the preparation of a spell parallels the preparation of a ritual (a ritual is, after all, a much more in-depth way of achieving a very similar result). As an example of a spell being created, throughout this chapter I have used the "Blessing for Safe Travel," the full text of which can be found in the Grimoire of Enchantment Magick in Chapter Nine.

The intention...

The intention of the spell is simply a short description of what should be achieved by its successful and honest casting. For example, "To protect travelers from harm as they journey from place to place."

You need to consider the ethical and moral implications of the new spell. It's all very well to create a spell for your specific needs, but remember that once it has been written down it will probably be used again — most likely by other people as well — at some time in the future. Take some time to examine your intentions in the light of both the Sorcerer's Code and the Wiccan

Rede. If the intention isn't pure by those standards, it would be worth double-checking your reasons for creating the spell in the first place. As a rule, if you wouldn't mind somebody else casting the spell, and you wouldn't mind being affected by it yourself, there's no harm in creating it. Otherwise, you may find yourself with an ethical dilemma when you come to use the new spell later on!

And don't forget to consider the possible consequences of the magick you are planning. Remember the Law of Cause and Effect (known as the Karma principle, and the Law of Return)? When you use magick to change something here and now, somewhere later on there will be an equal reaction. You don't want to cause that avalanche effect and end up with a chain reaction coming back at you, or change anything here and now that could cause an unforeseen chain reaction of its own. Although it seems daunting to consider every possibility, the best you can do is to look conscientiously for any problems or undesired results that might arise from the spell. In other words, avoid those spells that might have uncontrolled or unpredictable effects.

Physical preparations...

Because a spell is cast by a concentrated effort of the mind, it is important that your mind, body, and spirit are all as relaxed and at ease as possible before the spell is cast. Of course, other factors also come into play when casting a spell: your physical location and surroundings can play a vital role in setting your frame of mind, and in the formation of the magick itself. Sometimes it helps to be in physical contact with the spell's subject (the recipient of the magic, whether a human, an animal, or an inanimate object). At other times you may find that your spell is best cast at a distance.

Use the Physical Preparations section to instruct the magick user how to find the best location, surroundings, timing, and astrological (or astronomical) times for their magick. This is also the place to make sure that any special preparations are mentioned — for example, some arcane spells might require magick users to remove any watches, jewelry, or mechanical devices from their body first.

Besides those preparations, there's the mind and spirit to consider as well. Some spells may be designed to be cast under stressful circumstances (such as spells that cause persuasion or sedation), but those are very rare. The majority of spells are designed to be cast with a clear and untroubled mind. When you write your new spell, it is worth urging the reader to use some kind of mental and spiritual relaxation technique — perhaps a simple yoga exercise, a meditation, or a repetitive chant. I find that repeating the Divine Prayer for a while helps me to focus my attention and clear my mind of other thoughts and worries. The Divine Prayer appears on page 1 of this book.

In the case of the "Blessing for Safe Travel," the magick users are told that they need to be able to touch, see, or hear each person to whom the spell applies (or, in a pinch, have access to a witness of any persons not present).

Magickal preparations...

The magick that is brought about by the spell will be heavily influenced by a huge variety of conditions, some of which may coincide with each other. You need to provide as much detail as you can in this section to help magick users cast the spell most effectively.

When you consider the types of magickal preparation you might cover, try to think of likely situations in which the spell would be used. That should help you to identify the reasons, times, seasons, or other magicks that could be involved.

Is any other magick already acting on the subject? If so, the spell may need to be adjusted on the spot to avoid unwanted side effects or interference. The positions of the sun, moon, planets, and stars are also very significant in the casting of lots of common spells. As you will remember, the moon's effect when it is waxing tends to reinforce "positive" ideas and suggestions (such as increasing strength), while the waning phase tends to reinforce "negative" intentions (like reducing the effects of stress). The day of the week, month, and year can also be significant magickally. You can use the seasons of the year very effectively with magickal forces: spring for strengthening, summer for reinforcing, autumn for decreasing, and winter for stopping the magick.

The "Blessing for Safe Travel" would be best cast on a Wednesday, because that day of the week is associated with Mercury, which is the controlling planet for travel, speed, and flight. It doesn't really matter whether the moon is waxing or waning, because either aspect can be used to the spell's advantage (a waxing moon could reinforce the safety aspect of the spell, while a waning moon could decrease the likelihood of any mishap along the way). In the case of this particular spell, the seasons of the year aren't relevant, because the journey might be at any time of year. Your magickal preparation section for this spell would therefore make the point that the spell is best cast on a Wednesday, and also would point out the best ways of using the moon's influence (whether waning or waxing).

The enchantment...

The enchantment is the part of the spell that others will see happening — it's the part that you normally speak, chant, or sing aloud. Of course, if your psychic abilities allow, you may choose to invoke the spell's shape in your mind by the power of thought and mental visualization alone, in which case nobody is likely to realize you're casting a spell — which may be useful!

Here you will lay out the exact script and give instructions on speaking, chanting, or singing the spell into being. You will certainly find that rhyming and rhythmic verse have more of an effect on the mind than non-rhyming and non-rhythmic phrases. An amazing number of well-known poems could be (and indeed have been) taken straight off the page and used as spells — for relaxation, love interests, and the like!

To empower the spell, the most common method is a simple statement of personal assertion, such as "So mote it be!" (literally meaning "Let it be done as I have said!"), which is generally followed by the drawing of a pentagram in the air, to seal and protect the spell.

For the "Blessing for Safe Travel," I decided to go for a combination of rhyming and non-rhyming, rhythmic and non-rhythmic verse. I didn't want the spell to have a heavy feel to it, but thought it should be fairly light and short. I also opted for a kind of "Olde English" (perhaps even Gothic) feel in the wording, more for dramatic appeal than anything else. There's absolutely nothing to stop you using any language or style you choose, but it helps if your subject can understand what you're saying.

For centuries past, and even today to a limited extent, some magick users have adopted Latin as their language of spells and rituals. Latin is very impressive to hear, but most subjects don't understand a word of it — which can cut away a certain degree of the spell's effectiveness.

It is also good to include exact details about how many subjects can be affected by a single casting of the spell (which, in the case of this blessing spell, is just one person at a time).

After you have written the script for the spell itself, indicate somehow that the spell is finished, so that the magick user knows for sure that the job is done (even if it's only a single line saying "The spell is complete").

Final actions...

Although you can now assume that the spell has been successfully cast, there are usually one or two loose ends to tie up afterwards. In some cases, the subjects may need to take a particular course of action (or make a personal assertion) to allow the spell work effectively for them. In other cases, the magick user may need to carry out a task or provide the subjects with some instructions to follow. This final section of the spell script is a good place to describe what needs to be done, if anything. Quite often, if a spell uses only one or two of the five elements, the magick user may well end up with unbalanced body energies: in such cases, it is wise to include a note about "grounding" him- or herself as a final action.

For the "Blessing for Safe Travel," there's no particular need for grounding because the spell is very simple. There is, however, something to be done for the subject. If your budget allows, it is a thoughtful gesture to give the subject a pentagram pendant or charm as a token reminder of the sealed magickal protection. Pendants bearing the likeness of St. Christopher are often associated with safe travel, even by pagan folk, despite his obviously Christian origins.

When you have drawn up your complete spell script, go back over each section and double check the instructions, wording, and information you have provided. Always test the spell and achieve full success with it before you commit it to your Book of Shadows and Enchantments. If you can't cast the spell successfully yourself, there's every chance that it won't work no matter who tries to cast it. And, as pointed out previously, be sure to check spelling, punctuation, and grammar, and make sure that there are no ambiguities that could lead to confusion.

COMPLETING THE SPELL

Arguably, the most important factor when setting out to cast any kind of magick is the state of your mind at the time. Regardless of whether the magick being cast is high, low, small, arcane, shadow, enchantment, white or black, you need a calm, controlled, and purposeful mind. It is vital that this message is somehow conveyed, either directly or more subtly, in the writing of your spell script.

I tend to write up new spells, like my ritual scripts, with a simple and easy-to-read layout. The spell is divided into the sections already covered here, and the text is written without any unnecessary or overcomplicated words or jargon. When writing a spell script, the aim is to create something that can be read, understood, and used by anybody at any time, so the use of buzzwords and catchphrases won't help anyone. It's best to avoid abbreviations, unless they are clearly noted somewhere in your Book of Shadows and Enchantments. Personal experience shows that spells are easier to use when the author has written them as if speaking directly to the reader, using phrases like "You'll find it easier to..." rather than "It is easier to..."

A vital point that is often missed is that when you write your spell, you already know the full background of the situation at hand. You know why the spell was created, and exactly what circumstances it perfectly addresses. Don't forget that somebody else who reads your script later may not fully understand your reason for creating the spell in the first place. Think of future readers as people you've never met, and don't assume they know everything that you do.

Try to put in explanatory notes or comments about things in the spell that others may later wonder about, too. Explain anything that could cause someone to ask "Why?" — and make it obvious which words are your narrative and which are to be spoken aloud. If you're writing the script by hand, perhaps use different color inks (but make sure you can see the colors in dim light) or, if using a computer or typewriter, try different type styles and sizes. It may seem like a huge task but, with a little careful planning, a new spell can be a real joy to create.

CHAPTER 6

PSYCHIC ENHANCEMENT

HOW DO PSYCHIC PHENOMENA WORK?

O f all the parts of the physical human body, nothing is closer to the aethereal realm than the thoughts of the physical mind. Thoughts are a form of vibrational energy that is usually seen as being restricted to the space occupied by the human brain. Looking at other forms of vibrational energy, such as radio or television wave transmissions, you can see that vibrational energy is very efficient at traveling long distances, even through solid matter, with very little interference. The thoughts of the physical mind are closely linked to the thoughts (vibrational energies) of the aethereal counterpart of the human body — that which we've already come to know as the life force or spirit. The process of thought is the one function of the human body that can quite easily bridge the gap between the physical and aethereal realms. Now remember that the physical realm is limited by time and geography, but the aethereal realm is not. Well, if your spirit can access information from any place or any time, there's no reason why your physical mind shouldn't be able to access some of those vibrations. Some people seem to have a natural aptitude for this kind of psychic ability, while others have to practice hard to achieve the same effect. Either way, it is well within everyone's reach, without exception!

That's how psychic ability normally works. In simple terms, it's the ability to turn aethereal vibrations into thought patterns that the physical mind can understand and interpret accurately. There is, however, one small complicating factor that makes it very difficult to pin down an exact psychic thought transfer taking place: The human mind is also an exceptionally powerful computation device, which analyzes and collates information at an amazing speed, processing and filtering information rapidly in light of what it believes to be true. In the unconscious mind, logic is rapidly applied to any thought conceived, and if the thought does not conform to past experience, the mind will try to filter and adjust the thought to fit an existing pattern before it allows the thought to rise to consciousness. Medically speaking, there are hundreds of well-known and easily identified areas of the brain and nervous system that filter information and block out the parts that don't seem to make sense. The key to using your psychic ability is being able to suspend the brain's filtering and conformity functions, and to allow thoughts to surface into your consciousness without any tampering along the way. That's what takes so much practice!

Some people have what they call psychic intuition, and for some reason it's more often women than men, perhaps giving rise to what we call "female intuition." The word "intuition" comes from the Latin *intueri* and means "instinctive knowledge of or belief about something without conscious reasoning." That fits right in: the mind picks up an unconscious thought or image that comes from the aethereal mind, which knows and sees things without the barriers of geography or time, and that thought somehow surfaces into consciousness without the mind's getting a chance to damage it first.

USING PSYCHIC ABILITIES IN SORCERY

Here's the interesting part: that same process works even more effectively in reverse. Let your physical mind decide what it wants to suggest to — or share with — your aethereal mind and form it into a clear thought or image in your mind. Instantly, your spirit has access to that thought, because your spirit doesn't need to process out all sorts of unwanted chemical impulses — it doesn't have any! Your spirit can hear every thought of your mind and knows your physical body more intimately than your physical mind does. This is because your physical mind is so limited in what it can cope with at a given moment that it needs to concentrate only on the things that seem most important to it at the time. Your spirit has no such restriction and can understand things that are way beyond human reckoning without any problem. The reason your mind doesn't automatically share your spirit's vast knowledge is that it simply can't handle that much information. The physical mind is a coordinator of the physical body — it's our interface to the physical world around us.

There's a very useful side effect of this ability to transfer vibrational energies (in the form of thoughts and feelings) from the physical to the aethereal and vice versa. It enables a vibrational energy created by Person A in Place 1, to be received instantly by Person B in Place 2. In fact, that is what is known as telepathic communication or telepathy. It uses the aethereal realm to bridge the gaps in space (and potentially time, too) to send energy and vibrations to any place at any time. The only condition is that Person A and Person B need to be in some form of vibrational harmony with each other. It's just like using a telephone: you need to know and use the right phone number to reach the other person! You can achieve this most easily by using a witness — a photograph, lock of hair, signature, and so on — of the intended recipient of the energy.

The implications for magick are quite astonishing. When you use these psychic abilities, you are automatically able to perform Attuned Harmonic Mind Magick. In much the same way as people send and receive telepathic messages, it is a simple matter to send (or receive) telepathic magick too. Remember that magick operates on the aethereal plane, so it's right at home there. When you're casting magick using a witness of the recipient, you're already using Attuned Harmonic Magick of a kind. The difference with Attuned Harmonic Mind Magick is that you're establishing a direct spiritual link between yourself and the recipient and plunging the magick straight into it, like with a hypodermic needle.

A word of warning: The benefits are obvious: very little can interfere; there will never be any power loss between you and the recipient, and nobody else can be affected by mistake. The dangers are perhaps less obvious, though; you're opening up a channel between yourself and the recipient (this is sometimes known as channeling), and you may be overpowered if the recipient is carrying something that's stronger than you are. There's also the danger that if the recipient is carrying a spiritually originated ailment, you may become tainted by it yourself while you're linked up. You need to make sure that you have some kind of spiritual protection set up (such as a magick circle) or at the very least have some method of spiritual cleansing or grounding at your disposal immediately afterwards.

PRACTICE SESSION: PSYCHIC TRAINING

There are a number of ways in which you can develop or improve your psychic abilities, and if you're willing to discipline yourself to do these exercises, you should make rapid progress. Most of us have never learned to use the amazing capacity of our minds for this purpose, and so, as with any muscle-building exercise, your progress may seem slow to begin with. Don't let that discourage you; these exercises have been tried, proven, and used over thousands of years in cultures all across the world, and have proven very successful with only one exception: those who give up.

Train yourself regularly

This training section is not intended to be a "once only" session. You'll need to keep doing these exercises on a regular (preferably daily) basis until the principles of the use of psychic ability become second nature to your mind. The human brain learns information permanently only after much repetition. In general, it takes about seven repetitions for the brain to form a neural pathway that enables itself to carry information permanently. Once this pathway has been formed, the brain apparently needs to refresh it only every ten years or so. In other words, after you repeat an exercise enough times, it becomes a part of you.

Take note...

It is best to keep a small notebook in which you can record the exercises you have carried out each day, along with how successful you were. Don't feel self-conscious about keeping track of your progress, and there's certainly no need to feel guilty if you don't end up practicing as regularly as you intend to. The important thing is to keep trying and not give up on it. If you feel that you're "wasting your time" during a session, stop the session and begin again the next day. It's very important that you feel like doing the practice session, because you won't be able to marshal yourself properly if there's something else you would rather be doing!

Be patient and steadfast...

The exercises here are set in a specific order for a good reason. The best way to approach them is to fully master exercise number 1 before even trying exercise number 2, and so on. The reasoning behind that approach is simple: you'll find that each exercise uses some or all of the skills learned in the exercises before it. To attempt the exercises in any other order, although it isn't impossible, will be significantly more difficult. While you may already have mastered the skills for some of the early exercises, it still won't hurt to run through them first, just to ease yourself into the remaining exercises. As a rule, I would suggest that practice sessions last no more than about half an hour, because it can sometimes seem a little tedious after that. Finally, don't do more than one exercise on any given day — just do one until you're happy with your progress, and then stop for the day.

Exercise 1 — Thought control

This first exercise is a very simple one that is designed to teach the art of patience and determination. You must be able to control what your mind is doing in ordinary circumstances before you can consider letting it have complete control over something as potentially dangerous as magick! The first thing to realize is that your mind is probably used to doing what it wants to do, rather than what it needs to do. The human mind, if it has not already been trained, is essentially undisciplined. The phrase "attention span" is often used to describe the length of time your mind can concentrate solely on one theme. With the advent of television's ten-minute commercial break scheme, the average attention span is now less than ten minutes.

Another television phenomenon has been observed scientifically in recent years: channel hopping. That happens when you allow your mind to demand something new every few seconds! Although magick is not limited by time, the human mind is! So first, try this simple exercise until you can guarantee yourself at least a ten-minute, uninterrupted attention span.

An initial experiment: Sit down with your notebook and a pen. Set an alarm or timer to stop you after five minutes so you don't have to keep watching the clock. Now think of nothing in particular for five minutes, letting your thoughts wander freely. It doesn't matter what you think about. When the five minutes are up, quickly recall and write down as many of the subjects that you thought about as you can. Now get a calculator and divide the number 300 by the number of things you thought about, and that's your attention span measured in seconds.

Part One: Set a timer for ten minutes, sit down, and close your eyes. Pick a word or phrase that you know well and keep that one single thought in your mind. Hold it there for the whole ten minutes, without deviating from it. It's hard at first, but this is essential. If you fail, note down the date and the length of time you managed; then reset the timer and try again. That will act as an encouragement as you slowly improve.

Part Two: Do this only when you have perfected Part One. Set the timer for ten minutes, sit down, and close your eyes. Clear your mind completely and simply stare into the blackness of your mind for the whole ten minutes. It's an unnerving experience at first, but you'll get used to it quite quickly. As always, if you fail, make sure you note down the date and the length of time you managed.

Exercise 2 — Self-awareness

What to do: This exercise only takes one session and doesn't require too much effort. On the other hand, it does require almost brutal honesty with yourself. You've got to know where your own strengths and weaknesses lie in order to be able to work with or against them in the future. Sit down with your note-book and make a page called Strengths, and another page called Weaknesses. Now think carefully about all the things you like about yourself, your personality, and your attitudes. Write them all down on the Strengths page. Do the same for things you don't like about yourself and write them on the Weaknesses page. Don't fool yourself into thinking that you've got very few weaknesses: if you're in any doubt as to that, try asking a few of the people you work or socialize with (but don't expect to like them after they finish telling you what they think!). If you ever happen to come up with other things, or decide that something about you has changed, come back to these pages and revise them. Keep them up to date. You'll be amazed at how much you change.

Exercise 3 — Breathing and relaxation

Part One: Set the timer for five minutes. Sit down, close your eyes, and think of a short-term goal for yourself. Perhaps you want to eat less or give up something like smoking, or maybe you just want to be happier or more positive in life. Whatever the goal is, make sure you can achieve it without outside help.

Keep that goal in your mind for the whole five minutes. If your mind wanders at all, reset the timer and start again. Keep doing this until you've held the thought for the full five minutes, then proceed immediately to Part Two.

Part Two: Set the timer for five minutes again. Slowly take a deep breath and fill your lungs until they almost hurt. Then breathe out again at a comfortable rate. Don't go over the top on deep breathing or you'll hyperventilate (too much oxygen in the bloodstream)! If that happens, have a paper bag handy. Put the bag over your mouth and breathe slowly in and out of it so that you aren't breathing in any new oxygen.

Relax and get comfortable. Then slowly breathe deeply in and out. With each breath inward, think of that goal you wanted to achieve, and with each breath outward, clear your mind completely. Keep this up for five minutes if possible. You will need to repeat Parts One and Two together regularly until you develop the control needed to breathe deeply for the full five minutes.

Part Three: When you have completed Parts One and Two together, get your notebook and write down the date along with the goal you chose to work toward. Continue doing this exercise daily for at least a week (or seven times), while keeping a close eye on your personal progress toward your goal. Prepare to be amazed. You've already used your most basic psychic ability — the affirming power of the mind.

Exercise 4 — Mind and body harmony

The first time around: Don't set the timer for this one, but make sure you have plenty of time and that you aren't going to be interrupted. Silence the telephone, close the curtains, hang out the "Do Not Disturb" sign! Lie down somewhere comfortable and not too cold. Relax your body and, most important, keep your eyes open (otherwise you might fall asleep). Think about relaxing each and every set of muscles, starting at your toes. Some of your muscles have to keep working to maintain your body (like your heart, and the diaphragm that inflates and deflates your lungs), but all the others have no excuse for even twitching. Pay special attention to relaxing any muscles that twitch or become uncomfortable. When you're fully relaxed, stay there for as long or as little as you like and then slowly get up and end the session for the day.

The second time onward: Set the timer for ten minutes and relax. Stay there until the ten minutes are up. With each session, increase the time by five minutes until you get to thirty minutes. When you can do that, your body will be sufficiently subject to your mind's authority, and you'll be ready for the next exercise.

Exercise 5 — Unconscious programming

Initial preparation: Decide on a short-term goal such as an improvement that you want to make in your personality — perhaps you want to smile more, or to lose your fear of heights. Carefully work out a sentence (in the form of a command to yourself) that expresses your goal without using negativity, or undefined time and space. In other words, avoid using words like: tomorrow, today, yesterday, next week, here, there, not, etc.

For example: Use "I will be happier with every passing day," rather than "I will not be unhappy tomorrow." Your unconscious mind immediately filters out things that you don't want to hear or that don't seem to apply, so words like "tomorrow" and "do not" never rank very high in priority. Get your notebook and write the date along with the sentence (so that you don't forget the exact wording).

What to do: This exercise session takes place just as you go to bed at night, so in many ways it is the easiest of them all! When you're about ready to try to get to sleep, read your goal command sentence from your notebook, then lie back, close your eyes, and hold that thought for as long as you can before allowing yourself to fall asleep. Your unconscious mind is always awake, so the best time to pass information to it is when your conscious mind is just going off to sleep. You'll need to do this exercise regularly for at least a week (or seven times) for each command that you want to issue.

Exercise 6 — Image-memory training

What to do: You're about to train your mind to observe and remember images accurately. Select five or six different objects and place them on a tray. Alternatively, find a large color photograph that shows several different objects. Now set your timer for five minutes, and sit down and look at the objects, trying to memorize their position, orientation, color, shape, and texture. When the five minutes are up, get your notebook, start a new page, and put the date at the top. Now quickly write down all that you can remember about the objects, perhaps even drawing a rough sketch of their positions on the tray. Do this exercise once for at least three sessions, rearranging or completely replacing the objects every time.

Exercise 7 — Sensory-memory training

Preparation: Next you'll train your mind to observe and remember other senses such as taste, smell, and sound. There are two parts to this exercise; complete both parts in each session. You'll need to find a food with a distinctive taste, another (different) food with a distinctive smell, and something that makes a noise. For example, I chose a banana for taste, an orange for smell, and a piece of paper to crumple up for the sound.

Part One: Taste the first food and savor it, exploring every aspect of the taste with your mouth. Make sure it reaches all your taste buds and get to know the flavor intimately — even more than you would if you were just eating the food as part of a meal. Now pick up the next food and smell it carefully. Take a deep breath of its aroma and get to know it. Now make the noise you chose and listen to it carefully, memorizing every last detail. Make the sound as many times as you need to in order to memorize it.

Part Two: Set the timer for five minutes. Sit down and close your eyes, and then concentrate on recalling first the taste, then the smell, and finally the sound. Bring them so clearly into your mind that you can imagine them being real again. Keep recalling them one after the other (but not at the same time) until the five minutes are up. When you've done this exercise successfully once, there's no need to repeat it unless you want to.

Exercise 8 — Image creation

Part One: You're about to teach your mind how to create permanent image memories from scratch. Set the timer for ten minutes. Sit down, close your eyes, and clear your mind completely. Imagine that your mind is a blank canvas on which you are about to paint a scene. Now imagine that you are looking at a scenic landscape — hills, dales, trees, river, blue sky, anything you want. The important thing is to keep it simple. Concentrate on the colors, depth, textures, light, and shadows. Make this scene into a color photograph in your mind. Keep the picture in your mind so that you can visualize every part of it, memorizing all the fine detail. When the time is up, proceed immediately to Part Two.

Part Two: Reset the timer for another five minutes. Close your eyes and clear your mind. Now try to recall as much of that picture as you can, rebuilding the whole color photograph, if possible. You may need to repeat this whole exercise from start to finish several times (over several sessions) before you can recall the complete image. When you are finally satisfied that you have the complete image, add a small white bird to it, flying across the picture from left to right, turning at the right-hand side and coming back again. Keep the bird flying back and forth, keeping the details of the picture intact in your mind, until the five minutes are up.

Exercise 9 — Sensory creation

What to do: Now you're going to teach your mind to create images and other senses at the same time. Set the timer for five minutes. Sit down, close your eyes, and clear your mind. Recall in detail again the scenic image that you created in the last exercise. Once again, add the flying bird to the otherwise static image. If there isn't already a stream in the picture, add one that flows away from the foreground out to the horizon. In your mind, imagine the sound of gently flowing water coming from the stream. Hear it sparkle and rush as it sweeps along its course toward the horizon. Keep the image, the flying bird, and the water sound going in your mind, not letting any of them slip out of focus. After the first few anxious moments (which may feel a bit like a mental juggling act), this should be a very relaxing experience. The aim is to feel almost as if you're actually there. After the five minutes are up, take a few minutes to let your mind relax a little.

Exercise 10 — Psychic programming

Preparation: Prepare a healthy meal for yourself and set it down on the table, ready to eat. You're going to transfer vibrational energy from your body into the food, carrying with it the notion that the food is going to be really beneficial to you, and that you'll feel more vital and strong after eating it. This is derived from an ancient form of food blessing ceremony, from which the dinner table "prayer of grace" also developed.

What to do: Hold your hands, palms facing downward, over the meal, and, in your mind, tell the food that it is good, healthy, vital food and that it is beneficial to you. It won't hurt to thank the Goddess for providing it, too! What you're doing now is establishing a psychic link between you and your subject — in this case, the food.

You've harmonized yourself with the food. Now go ahead and eat it, and enjoy it!

This principle can be applied to anything that you make use of, from water that you bathe in, to the fuel you put in your car, to the shovel you use to dig the garden. Just remember to be grateful and sincere; a harmonious life is less stressful all around.

Exercise 11 — Psychic prediction

Preparation: Your mind already knows how to work in harmony with your body. Your mind is already disciplined. Now you're going to teach it how to see the possibilities of the future.

Get three regular dice and place them on the table. Start a new page in your notebook and draw a line straight down the middle, dividing it into two equal columns. At the top of the left column, write the heading "Throws," and at the top of the right column, write "Correct."

What to do: Concentrate on the dice before you throw them. Imagine throwing them onto the table and then, in your mind's eye, take a look at the numbers that come up. Total up those three numbers and remember the result. Now make a mark in the "Throws" column and throw all three dice together; then total them up. Compare your real and imagined dice totals. If your imagined total is within one point either side of the real total, you can consider your imagined total to be correct, so make a mark in the "Correct" column; otherwise, don't. For example, if the real total is 16, and you imagined a total of 15, 16, or 17, then that's counted as correct. After every ten throws, draw a line across the page and compare how you are progressing based on the number of correct predictions out of every ten throws. With three dice, two correct throws out of every ten would be about average for pure chance. When you are maintaining a higher average than that, you know you're beating the odds and advancing in your psychic prediction abilities. Try this exercise for several sessions to help overcome the "but-that-might-just-have-been-luck" feeling.

Exercise 12 — Psychic intuition

Preparation: Get a deck of ordinary playing cards and remove any extra cards such as jokers, bridge cards, etc. Shuffle the pack well so there's no way of knowing which order the cards will be in. Keep the pack with the cards facedown at all times, and no peeking! Now take four cards out of the pack at random, still facedown, so that you can't see their values. Line them up on the table and you're ready to start.

Part One: Place your hand on each card in turn and try to visualize the hidden face of the card in your mind. There's no hurry, so take your time and be confident. You're bound to get it wrong to begin with, but as you practice you'll uncover psychic intuition that you've probably never really experienced before. At this stage, just try to see the color of the suit (red for diamonds and hearts, or black for spades and clubs). Write down your predictions in your notebook and then turn the cards over to see how many you got right. Keep a record in the notebook so that you can see your improvement over time. When you begin to get all four right almost every time, move on to Part Two. Part One may take several sessions to complete successfully.

Part Two: Put the cards back in the deck, shuffle them again, and take four new cards. Follow the same procedure as before, but this time try to see the actual suit (hearts, diamonds, spades, or clubs) of each card. Make notes as before. When you start getting them all right almost every time, move on to Part Three. Part Two may take several sessions to complete successfully.

Part Three: Put the cards back in the deck, shuffle them again, and take four new cards. Follow the same procedure as before, but this time try to see not only the suit (hearts, diamonds, spades or clubs) of each card but also whether it is a number card or picture card (Jack, Queen, or King). Make notes as before. When you start getting them all right almost every time, move on to Part Four. Part Three may take several more sessions to complete successfully.

Part Four: Put the cards back in the deck, re-shuffle them, and take just one new card. This time you're aiming to see both the suit and the value (Ace, 2, 3, 4, 5, 6, 7, 8, 9, 10, Jack, Queen, or King). Make notes as before. When you start getting it right almost every time, you've embarked on a very exciting road of psychic intuition and prediction.

These exercises aren't only for the beginner; they'll help keep your skills sharpened to perfection, even after you have years of experience behind you. Always keep practicing and never let your mind get lazy.

Exercise 13 — Psychic telepathy

Preparation: You're going to need to work with somebody else here, and whoever you choose will need to be just as patient as you are (possibly more so!). It is also important that he/she follows your instructions to the letter! You'll both need notepads and somewhere to sit where you can't see each other. Sitting back to back will be okay.

What to do: Your assistant has the easier job: to think of a number from 1 to 10, write it on the notepad (as proof of the number), clear the mind completely, and concentrate purely on that number. Make sure your assistant realizes that he/she doesn't have to try to somehow "transmit" it to you, but just concentrate on the number. Your job is more interesting: Sit down, clear your mind, and concentrate not on numbers but on your assistant's mind. Try to visualize your mind and his/hers merging into one consciousness, so that the conscious thoughts of one become the conscious thoughts of the other. As you do, impressions will begin to enter your mind; if there's a number (from 1 to 10) among them, say it aloud. At this point your assistant can tell you the original number. Keep a record of that original number and your impression number on your notepad. After every ten attempts draw a line across the page so that you can chart your increasing success. Statistically speaking, you'd only get one out of every 10 guesses right if you were relying on chance. Anything better than that and you're already into telepathic territory.

Future experimentation: This isn't part of the exercise but it might be worth doing later on if your assistant is willing. Why not try, first of all, guessing numbers from a greater range, say from 1 to 100 instead? Once you have become proficient at that (and you will), you could move on to sets of words, images, or phrases. If you work hard to improve your telepathic skills, your achievements can be amazing: reading thoughts and feelings, emotions, even sensing ulterior motives that others try to hide from you! It's just a matter of commitment and practice.

Exercise 14—Psychic magick

What to do: You're about to teach your mind to send magick directly from you to somewhere (or someone) else! Pick a small, harmless spell that you can remember casting successfully at some point in the past. Now recall your feeling of satisfaction as you sent the spell off into the aether. Recall your feeling of pleasure when you realized that your spell had worked exactly as you wanted. Hold your hands out in front of you as if you were cupping them around a tennis ball. Now take that powerful feeling that embodies the spell's shape and the satisfaction of knowing that it is done, and visualize aetheric energy coming from your hands. Make it into a ball of aether between your hands, keeping it in your mind's eye, visualizing it constantly, without wavering. You will find that if you slowly and carefully remove your hands from around the ball, it will stay there — hovering in the air in front of you. Now start to feed more of your energy into the ball and let it grow a little more. If after a few minutes the ball hasn't already turned white, then gently will it to do so, feeding it your own aetheric energy as you go. When the ball has reached about the size of a football, you're ready to send it on its way. Picture, in your mind, the subject or recipient of the spell. Picture the ball appearing in that picture, and disappearing from in front of you. Finally, in your mind, instruct the ball to go and fulfil its destiny. Allow it to vanish. It is done!

When your mind is strong and obedient enough, you will find that you don't have to recall a spell that has already been done, but you will be able to confidently create the right magickal shapes as you need them. That's what's known as Psychically Enhanced Magick. The most important thing to remember is that — particularly with things of the mind where you can't always physically see what's happening — you have to practice to learn and then you have to keep doing it to stay at the peak of your newfound ability.

CHAPTER 7

THE HIGHEST INITIATION

WHAT IS THE HIGHEST INITIATION?

The Highest Initiation is the penultimate of the eight steps of apprenticeship in the Craft of Sorcery — those being: the call, searching, researching, experimentation, initiation, apprenticeship, high initiation, and finally, mastery of magick.

By now you have learned and experienced all that you need in order to decide whether you want to follow sorcery as your chosen craft. This initiation is not a personal commitment to yourself, but a commitment to sorcery in the presence of the Goddess herself. The initiation involves your being recognized as a dedicated sorcerer by the Lady. Because of the presence of the Goddess, the Highest Initiation takes the form of a ritual that includes the casting of a magick circle for your protection.

WHEN SHOULD YOU DO IT?

This could be the most difficult decision you will ever have to make. You are entering into sorcery as a dedicated way of life and spiritual growth and, though it isn't impossible to change your mind, you need to consider your commitment carefully. Don't enter into any High Initiation lightheartedly, just because you can give it up later. The Goddess is to be treated with respect and sincerity at all times — or else face the possibility of Her displeasure. Remember the Three-fold Law of Return? Well, the Goddess works in much the same way, but without stopping at three: whatever you show Her, she will show you in abundance! Treat the Lady honestly, and she will never fail you. Treat the Lady with insincerity, and she will treat you with indifference. I think you get the general idea. The point is that you should only undergo the Highest Initiation into sorcery when you know, beyond doubt, that you are committed to it and ready to begin your newfound way of life and spiritual development. Unlike other traditions such as witchcraft, sorcery tends to be a solitary path and is not normally subject to minimum periods of time between the various stages of development. For example, a witch coven may insist that new disciples should be educated in their tradition for at least a year before their first initiation. This obviously isn't the case for the lone sorcerer. The danger is that you might race through your education too quickly, in which case nothing much would happen and disillusionment would rapidly set in. Alternatively, you might work too slowly through the stages of development with a similar result. Keep your interest in development and progression alive by studying earnestly, practicing diligently, and regularly stretching the limits of your abilities.

WHAT EFFECTS CAN IT HAVE?

The effects of the Highest Initiation can be very few or very many, depending on how far you have already progressed by the time you decide to make your long-term commitment. In some cases, the most significant change may be a boost in your personal confidence, thanks to your new status as a Sorcerer, third degree. In many cases, it is not uncommon for knowledge, wisdom, magickal abilities, and psychic abilities to develop rapidly, almost as if "by magic," as they say. Two possible reasons are offered for this amazing increase in ability, and both are equally reasonable (although sadly there's no obvious way of telling which, if not both, has actually taken place). First, you may have received a blessing of might from the Lady in preparation for some divine task or purpose yet to be revealed. Second, you may have regained access to the might you have already accumulated in a previous incarnation. For example, you may have already been an experienced sorcerer in a past life.

There are two significant warnings to heed:

❖ The first is that your third degree title does not give you super-status or superiority over any other being, physical or aethereal, living or dead. To treat anyone or anything as your inferior or servant is the same as treating the Goddess with the same disrespect, because we were all brought forth equally from Her and will all return equally to Her in the end.

❖ The second warning is that the forces of nature (and the balance of energies throughout Creation) will not tolerate the destruction of any naturally sustained system. Such imbalances will inevitably result in the natural balance being restored by force. Take a look at what happens when humankind strips trees from rain forests and pollutes the waters and the air with toxic chemical compounds; nature begins to reestablish its balance with unstoppable force and will continue until the cause of the problem is eliminated. The same rules apply to magick (if not more so) and in the aethereal realms, so be careful to consider not only your motives but the consequences of your actions.

THE HIGHEST INITIATION

The ritual is made up of six major stages that need to be worked in order. Stage One involves the casting of a magick circle of protection. Stage Two is a simple self-blessing (attuning yourself to, and meeting with, the Goddess herself). Stage Three is the actual highest initiation ceremony. In Stage Four you perform a "high blessing" (a consecration for holy service) of your tools of the Craft. Stage Five is the enchantment of three cords of power that will act as a reserve of power for use later, should you need it. Finally, Stage Six is simply the breaking of the magick circle.

Equipment and ingredients...

For the casting of a circle of protection, you will need:
   ❖ an athame
   ❖ a soft rope of 260 inches (about 6.5m) or more in length
   ❖ a white candle with an appropriate stand or support
   ❖ a glass containing some pure water
   ❖ a glass containing some pure salt
   ❖ a dark mirror (in a pinch, a silver mirror wrapped up in black cloth)

For the high blessing of the tools of the Craft, you will need:
   ❖ the athame, and any other tools, to be blessed
   ❖ a symbol of initiation (such as a pentagram) to be worn close to your body

For the enchantment of the three cords of power, you will need:
- ❖ three narrow, natural cords thirteen inches (32.5cm) long
- ❖ a suitable sturdy box, bag, or cloth for their safe containment.

Physical preparations...

Before beginning the ritual, make sure you remove, hide, or cover all keepers of time (clocks, watches, and so forth). Remove all unnecessary clothing within reason, comfort, and prudence. It will also help to darken, to the greatest degree possible, the space in which you will be working.

Magickal preparations...

Work at any new or full moon, preferably at night and surrounded by nature. Make efforts to work undiscovered, uninterrupted, and in a silent place.

It is a good idea to take a personal magickal name that you will use to refer to yourself, both in rituals and in your dealings with others in the Craft. Doing so provides you with an opportunity to express your true self and your aspirations as a sorcerer. Your magickal name can be as imaginative or as down-to-earth as you like, and doesn't need to have anything in common with your real name. Many witches choose names that are rooted in nature itself (Bramble, Leaflight, and Twoherbs, to name some of my favorites). Sorcerers often take more far-fetched names, such as Starguide and Elfin, while others take jocular names like Gandalf and even Papa Smurf! It's up to you.

Stage One — The Casting of a Circle of Protection

Perform the "Making a Magick Circle" ritual (see page 73) to create a protective area for your Highest Initiation. When you cast the magick circle, make sure that you've got all your tools and equipment with you, ready for the ritual ahead. Make sure that you've read the complete script through so that you don't miss any vital details — there's nothing more annoying than having to stop the whole ritual halfway through because the three cords are sitting on the floor outside the circle!

After you have finished casting the circle, use the remaining water to anoint both the tip of your athame and the top of your head, declaring aloud your personally taken magickal name.

You may also choose to anoint any other magickal tools that are within the circle (except for the mirror and the candle). Remember: Don't leave, penetrate, break, or disturb the circle in your efforts to reach other items! It is not safe to do so at this point.

Stage Two — Self-Blessing — Attuning to the Goddess

Begging the Goddess's attention...
Stand in the middle of the circle, holding (in your left hand) the glass containing the remaining consecrated salt-water, and utter:
> Bless me, Mother, for I am Thy child.

Now dip the first two fingers of your right hand into the consecrated salt-water, and anoint your eyes, uttering:
> Blessed be my eyes, that I may clearly see Thy path.

Anoint your nose, uttering:
> Blessed be my nose, that I may breathe of Your essence.

Anoint your mouth, uttering:
> Blessed be my mouth, that I may speak of Thee.

Anoint your breast, uttering:
> Blessed be my breast, that I may be faithful in my works.

Anoint your loins, uttering:
> Blessed be my loins, which bring forth the life
> of humanity as Thou hast brought forth all Creation.

Finally, anoint your feet, uttering:
> Blessed be my feet, that I may always walk in Thy ways.

Pause for thought...
It is wise to pause to consider that you have requested the Goddess's personal attention at this time. Take time to savor this privileged moment before continuing...

Stage Three — The Highest Initiation

The testing of your soul...
Stand in the middle of the circle, facing East, and utter:
> I am a seeker [state your magickal name],
> Proven by Magick, I desire to attain

> *To high level within this Ancient Craft,*
> *And to delve within the deepest of Mysteries.*
> *I am willing now to begin the High Quest.*
> *In this initiation I surrender to symbolic death,*
> *To tests and purifications of the soul.*
> *I will be born once again with new portals opened,*
> *And new powers within my soul.*
> *But for now, I sleep the dreamless sleep.*

Pause for the space of thirteen heartbeats, or for the count of thirteen. Now make the sign of the pentacle on your forehead with the first finger of your right hand; then blow gently on that finger and utter:

> *By air my spirit goes forth*
> *Into realms strange and distant.*
> *By air shall my very soul be tested.*

Gently touch the candle or pass your right hand above the flame, and utter:

> *By fire, red and flaming,*
> *And not of this world*
> *Shall all dross be burned away.*
> *By fire shall my very soul be tested.*

Take up the glass of consecrated salt-water and anoint your forehead and your breast once again, uttering:

> *By water shall all which is old and useless*
> *Be dissolved and washed away.*
> *With water, pure and Magickal,*
> *Does new life arise once more.*
> *By water shall my very soul be tested.*

The initiation of the Goddess...

Put down the glass, sit in the middle of the circle, and make yourself comfortable.

Pause for thirteen heartbeats, or for the count of thirteen. Then utter the words of this vision and see it in the darkness of your mind:

Now a vision comes forth to me
Which I perceive in magick realms.
My soul has passed the tests
And waits in the cold darkness
Of a great, ancient, and echoing hall.
For a time all is silent.
Then before me, upon a great throne
Grows a nimbus of colored light,
Glowing ever brighter.
And thereupon, in brilliance and warmth,
Appears the High Queen,
Whose attention I have sought.
She is clad in soft robes
Of deepest blue and glowing red.
Her hair is a stream of the brightest gold.
The eyes of the Lady
Are blue and shining as the sea.
She looks upon me, and through me,
Seeing all that is past,
And all that is to come.
She sees my hopes and dreams,
Then smiles and gives me Her blessing.
And the vision is gone
As I am whirled away from that place
In growing warmth and light,
For my life has begun once again.
So mote it be!

Now take the athame and stand up (slowly!) facing North. Use your athame to trace the sign of the pentagram in the air, and then an upward pointing triangle above the tip of the pentagram. Your high initiation (of the third degree) is complete.

Stage Four — High Blessing of the Tools of the Craft

Warnings...

Tools should be blessed only if they are made primarily from wood, stone, metal, or natural fibers. Do not perform this blessing on behalf of other magick users — they must do it themselves when they learn the Craft. Do not try to bless anything that will cause harm or pain when used, or that would break the Wiccan Rede, "An ye harm none, do what ye will."

Deciding on the tools...

Before you start, you must decide upon the lifetime of each tool and, if you want, a magickal name for each tool. A tool's lifetime may be any length of time from a few minutes up to your entire lifetime or even longer. When naming a tool, avoid using your own magickal name — although you could use a name derived from your own.

Honoring the elements...

Stand in the middle of the circle, facing North. Turn around sunwise three times, pausing at East, South, West, and North to bow to each quarter. When you reach North for the third time, sit down.

Blessing the tools...

Pick up each tool in turn, bringing its lifetime (and name, as appropriate) into your mind. For each individual tool, utter:

> *Thou of the elements*
> *Who know my wish*
> *To bless this aide*
> *For the Lady's service,*
> *Grant it now.*

When all the tools are blessed, stand up and bow to each quarter three times as before. Finally, sit down and utter:

> *My many thanks,*
> *Thou of the elements,*
> *For thy aid.*

Stage Five — The Enchantment — Three Cords of Power

Enchantment of the cords...

Sit in the middle of the circle, facing East. Place the three separated cords on the ground in front of you. Take up your athame and hold its tip in front of your face.

Breathe in slowly and deeply, envisioning pure white aetheric light being drawn from the edges of the circle into your body. Now breathe out slowly onto the athame's tip, envisioning this energy flowing from your body into the athame. Do this a total of nine times; then use the athame to make the sign of the pentacle in the air, uttering:

> *O Gracious Lady,*
> *In Thy Name*
> *Do I work this rite.*

Wrap the three cords loosely around the blade of your athame and visualize the aetheric energy flowing freely from the athame into the cords. When this is done, separate the cords and lay them down on the ground. Lay down your athame also.

Take up the first cord, tying a knot as you make each of these three utterances:

> *This is the Number One, and the spell is now begun.*
> *This is the Number Two, thus may the spell be true.*
> *This is the Number Three, may this light be kept for me.*

Put down the first cord and pick up the second, tying the knots as you utter:

> *This is the Number Four, may the spell be strengthened more.*
> *This is the Number Five, may the spell now come alive.*
> *This is the Number Six, thus the spell be fixed.*

Put down the second cord and pick up the third, tying the knots as you utter:

> *This is the Number Seven, may power through me be given.*
> *This is the Number Eight, may the power within be great.*
> *This is the Number Nine, may the spell wax strong with time.*

Put the cords together into the keep-safe bag, box, or cloth, and utter:
In the name of the Lady, so mote it be.

The three cords of power are bound into three knots each, holding captive the aetheric power raised within the protected initiation circle. You may undo these knots in times of urgent need and direct their released energies to any cause desired. Heed this, though: the cords carry your own power, so guard them well and use them sparingly; they are powerful indeed.

Stage Six — The Dissolving of the Magick Circle

Before you finish your Highest Initiation, carefully follow the "Breaking the Magick Circle" ritual (page 77). Dissolving the circle properly is the best way of safely dissipating and dispersing any unneeded energies and magickal forces that may have built up during the ritual.

When you have broken the circle, collect your tools and cords, wrap or pack them appropriately, tidy away any remaining equipment, and go forth and have a hearty meal!

THE DO-AND-DON'T NAG LIST

If you've undergone the Highest Initiation, you are indeed headed for great things to come. On the journey you are facing, there will be low times and high times, and in all circumstances there are traps into which the unsuspecting might fall. Although there's really no substitute for personal experience, here's my quick-fire nag list to help you find your way around the most common traps, instead of walking right into them, like many who have gone before you!

DON'T... give up if you don't make rapid progress initially.

DO... keep trying, even if it means doing something else for a while between tries.

DON'T... work magick that directly affects others without their permission.

DO... keep the Sorcerer's Code, the Wiccan Rede, and the Law of Return in mind.

DON'T... be selfish or put yourself before others.

DO... use magick for the good of all. Put the needs of others before your own.

DON'T... be proud of what you are. Don't let your title go to your head.

DO... be proud of who you are. Do let your progress encourage you and others.

DON'T... fall into the trap of thinking that you are powerful in your own right.

DO... thank the Goddess, the God, and the elements every time your magick works!

WHERE TO GO FROM HERE?

What next? You've reached this point and you're asking me? It's your destiny, and that means it's your decision now. My desire for you is that the Lady will bless you as a true and honest student of the Craft of Sorcery, and that She will keep you safe from all evil from this day unto eternity. Blessed be!

If you want to contact me to share your successes or concerns, ask questions, or share newfound knowledge, please feel free to write me through the publisher, who will pass on your correspondence. Although I may not be able to reply to every letter immediately, I will do my best to answer genuine and sincere letters as quickly as I can.

GRIMOIRE OF SHADOW MAGICK

Where did this grimoire come from?

The shadows (ritual outlines) in this grimoire of magick are derived from the Book of Shadows and Enchantments of the Beneviche Order of Sorcery. The Order was named after Benevich the Sorcerer — an Anglo-French spiritual guide and teacher of magick who lived in the 18th century. The Order is devoted to the development and collection of magickal teachings that fit with his original ideas.

You may find that you want to alter the wording or methods of the rituals to fit in with your own beliefs and practices. They all conform to tried-and-tested patterns that make it easy for you to change them to suit your needs.

You'll find that most of the rituals have been written up for you to cast for other people. In cases where you want to cast them for yourself and there are no specific instructions, just treat yourself in the same way you'd treat any other subject. If you need a witness (such as a photograph), use a photograph of yourself. And when the words to be spoken refer to the subject, just say "me" or your own name instead.

May your works be successful and your days in the Craft be long and fruitful. Blessed be!

INDEX OF SMALL SHADOWS

Finding a soul mate
A ritual to help find a soul mate.

Summoning rain
A ritual to summon rain, snow, or other precipitation to a specific location.

Banishing rain
A ritual to repel rain, snow, or other precipitation from a specific location.

Summoning winds
A ritual to summon winds of specific strength to a specific location.

Banishing winds
A ritual to repel specific high winds from a specific location.

Encouraging natural growth
A ritual to encourage the natural growth or regrowth of specific plant life.

Retarding natural growth
A ritual to discourage the natural growth of specific unwanted plant life (weeds).

Banishing insomnia
A ritual to help the sleepless get a good night's sleep.

FINDING A SOUL MATE

The intention...
To help find a soul mate.

Equipment needed...

❖ Any article (hair, photo, etc.) that is a witness of your subject (the magick's recipient). Even if you're performing the ritual for yourself, you'll still need this item.
❖ A new cord of thirteen inches (32.5cm) in length (the Ritual Cord).
❖ A red candle (the Ritual Candle) mounted in a candleholder.
❖ A cloth, bag, or carton sufficient to contain the witness, ritual candle, and cord.

For the casting of a magick circle, you are going to need at the very least:

- ❖ Your athame or wand for casting the circle.
- ❖ A white candle in a candleholder (and matches, or a lighter).
- ❖ A glass containing some water.
- ❖ A glass containing a thin layer of salt.
- ❖ A dark mirror (magick mirror or black mirror).

Physical preparations...

Make yourself conscious of the elements of creation that surround you rather than dwelling on the troubles and unrest of everyday life. If you have any unresolved arguments or emotional disagreements with anyone, do your best to resolve them before starting this ritual.

Try to relax, allowing your mind to clear before you begin. There are lots of ways of relaxing — some favorites are meditation, chanting, and quiet reflection. It might be helpful to quietly repeat the words of the Divine Prayer to yourself. You'll find it on the first page of this book.

Magickal preparations...

Cast the magick circle (see page 73). Make sure you have all the necessary tools and magickal ingredients with you inside the circle. You may use any alternative circle casting, if you so desire, or you may choose to perform the ritual under an alternative form of protection (such as an amulet, a protective spell, or a protected place).

Ritual instructions...

As soon the circle (or other protection) is complete, immediately light the ritual candle and allow a single drop of its wax to fall on the witness to form a permanent physical association between the candle and the subject. For the same reason, dip each end of the ritual cord into the wax that melts beneath the ritual candle's flame (being careful not to set the cord alight). As you make these wax bonds, utter:

> *Fire, Water, Earth, and Air,*
> *Come gather now for magick pure:*
> *Cord and Witness bonded strong,*
> *By wax this magick will endure.*

Take up your athame and wrap the cord around it three times, taking hold of both ends with one hand.

If the ritual is for somebody else, utter:

> *In the name of all that is Divine,*
> *In the name of all Creation,*
> *And in the name of Love itself,*
> *I ask that [state the name of your subject]*
> *Is now entwined in spirit with [his/her] soul mate.*
> *I ask you, fleet and powerful God,*
> *That their hunt will be shortened to days.*
> *I ask you, fair and loving Goddess,*
> *That the hunter and hunted are united.*
> *In your wisdom, Divine One,*
> *I ask for their union and happiness enduring.*

Or, if you are performing this ritual for yourself:

> *In the name of all that is Divine,*
> *In the name of all Creation,*
> *And in the name of Love itself,*
> *I ask that I am now entwined*
> *In spirit with my soul mate.*
> *I ask you, fleet and powerful God,*
> *That my hunt will be shortened to days.*
> *I ask you, fair and loving Goddess,*
> *That the hunter and hunted are united.*
> *In your wisdom, Divine One,*
> *I ask for a sure union*
> *And happiness enduring.*

Now breathe fire and air energies from your body into the athame and allow that energy to flow completely from the athame into the cord. Remove the cord and tie a single knot at one end. Then wind the cord back around the athame just twice this time, uttering:

> *So mote it be.*

Likewise, breathe water and earth energies from your body into the athame, and allow that energy to flow completely from the athame into the cord. Remove the cord and tie a single knot in the middle and then wind the cord back around the athame just once this time, uttering:

So mote it be.

Finally, breathe pure white aetheric energy from your body into the athame and allow that energy to flow into the cord as well. Remove the cord and tie a single knot at the remaining end, uttering:

So mote it be.

Now extinguish the ritual candle and wrap it up with the witness and the ritual cord in the cloth or bag. If you wish, you may now undertake any other magick that you need to perform while you are still magickally protected.

You may now break the magick circle (see page 77) or leave your protective area and ground yourself in order to keep your body energies balanced. A meal is highly recommended.

Final actions...

Place the wrapped witness and ritual candle in a box or cupboard where they can remain undisturbed for seven days. On the same day of the week, seven days later, unwrap them. Throw away, burn, or bury the witness and the ritual candle, and untie all three knots in the ritual cord. If the cord's knots are too tight to be undone easily, then simply burn the cord to destroy it. The magick will begin working when the knots are undone.

SUMMONING RAIN

The intention...

To summon rain, snow, or other precipitation to a specific location.

A word of warning: Manipulating weather patterns is a very serious matter. The consequences and repercussions of changing the course of nature could be devastating to the environment. Normally, the weather is governed by natural, physical processes that must take place to maintain delicate balances in the Earth's atmosphere. Changing the way those processes work may be the cause of far more damage than good!

Equipment needed...

Specifically for this ritual you will need the following items:

❖ A photograph or pencil outline drawing of a dark cloud of rain (or snow, etc.).

❖ A black or dark-colored candle (the Ritual Candle) mounted in a suitable holder.

For the casting of a magick circle, you are going to need at the very least:

❖ Your athame or wand for casting the circle.

❖ A white candle in a candleholder (and matches, or a lighter).

❖ A glass containing some water.

❖ A glass containing a thin layer of salt.

❖ A dark mirror (magick mirror or black mirror).

Physical preparations...

Write on the photograph (or drawing) the name or a description of the specific location to be affected. Before you begin, clear your mind of any thoughts that aren't relevant to the ritual. It is often helpful to say the Divine Prayer (see page 1).

Magickal preparations...

Cast the magick circle (page 73), making sure that you have all the necessary tools and magickal ingredients with you inside the circle. You may use any alternative circle casting if you so desire, or you may choose to perform the ritual under an alternative form of protection (such as an amulet, a protective spell, or a protected place).

Ritual instructions...

As soon the circle (or other protection) is complete, immediately light the ritual candle and allow a single drop of its wax to fall on the cloud photograph (or pencil drawing) to form a permanent physical association between the candle and the intended weather pattern. As you make this wax bond, utter:

> Fire, Water, Earth, and Air,
> For magick gather here this day:
> Thought and purpose bonded strong,
> By wax this magick has its way.

Take up your athame and breathe fire, water, earth, and air energies from your body into the athame. Touch the tip of the athame to the photograph (or drawing) and allow the energy to be released in force, uttering:

> Elements of Fire and Earth,
> I call upon your counterpart,

Elements of Air and Water,
I summon thee by Ancient Art.
Let waters pour from clouds above,
And feed the land until it's done.

Now breathe pure white aetheric energy from your body into the athame. Once again, touch the tip of the athame to the photograph (or drawing) and allow the energy to be released in force, uttering:

So mote it be!

You may now break the magick circle (or leave your protective area) and ground yourself in order to keep your body energies balanced. A meal is highly recommended.

Final actions...

Keep the photograph (or drawing) somewhere safe until the magick has run its full course, or until there has been enough precipitation from the skies! When you burn or bury the paper, the magick will cease functioning and the rains will stop.

BANISHING RAIN

The intention...

To repel rain, snow, or other precipitation from a specific location.

A word of warning: As with all other spells that affect the weather's natural processes, take a great deal of care with this one. Don't adjust the weather without considering the possible consequences — remember that every plant needs water to grow, and every living creature needs water to survive.

Equipment needed...

Specifically for this ritual, you will need the following items:

❖ A photograph or pencil outline drawing of the sun shining in a clear sky.

❖ A white or yellow candle (the Ritual Candle) mounted in a suitable holder.

For the casting of a magick circle, you are going to need at the very least:

❖ Your athame or wand for casting the circle.

❖ A white candle in a candleholder (and matches, or a lighter).

❖ A glass containing some water.

❖ A glass containing a thin layer of salt.

❖ A dark mirror (magick mirror or black mirror).

Physical preparations...

Write on the photograph (or drawing) the name or a description of the specific location to be affected. Before you begin the ritual, clear your mind of all worries and unnecessary thoughts. As an aid to this mental relaxation, try concentrating on the Divine Prayer (on page 1).

Magickal preparations...

Cast the magick circle a (page 73), making sure that you have all the necessary tools and magickal ingredients with you inside the circle. You may use any alternative circle casting if you so desire, or you may choose to perform the ritual under an alternative form of protection (such as an amulet, a protective spell, or a protected place).

Ritual instructions...

As soon the circle (or other protection) is complete, immediately light the ritual candle and allow a single drop of its wax to fall on the sunshine photograph (or pencil drawing) to form a permanent physical association between the candle and the intended weather pattern. As you make this wax bond, utter:

> Fire, Water, Earth, and Air,
> For magick gather here this day:
> Thought and purpose bonded strong,
> By wax this magick has its way.

Take up your athame and breathe fire, water, earth, and air energies from your body into the athame. Touch the tip of the athame to the photograph (or drawing) and allow the energy to be released in force, uttering:

> Elements of Air and Water,
> I call upon your counterpart,
> Elements of Fire and Earth,
> I summon thee by Ancient Art.

> *Make light and warmth and sun prevail,*
> *The clouds and waters now to fail.*

Now breathe pure white aetheric energy from your body into the athame. Once again, touch the tip of the athame to the photograph (or drawing) and allow the energy to be released in force, uttering:

> *So mote it be!*

You may now break the magick circle (or leave your protective area) and ground yourself in order to keep your body energies balanced. A meal is highly recommended.

Final actions...

Immediately burn or bury the photograph (or drawing) to allow the magick to take effect.

SUMMONING WINDS

The intention...

To summon winds of specific strength to a specific location.

A word of warning: When you summon winds using this spell, be especially careful to specify the right power and strength! Is there a good reason for calling forth the wind? The most obvious example of a good reason is to move or divert a bad weather system. Also examine the possible results of your spell: could anyone or anything be put at risk? If so, it may be better not to cast the spell.

Equipment needed...

Specifically for this ritual you will need the following items:

- ❖ A number of feathers tied together (the more feathers, the stronger the winds).
- ❖ A paper tag (attached to the feathers) on which you write the name or description of the location to be affected.
- ❖ A blue candle (the Ritual Candle) mounted in a suitable holder.

For the casting of a magick circle, you are going to need at the very least:

- ❖ Your athame or wand for casting the circle.
- ❖ A white candle in a candleholder (and matches, or a lighter).

❖ A glass containing some water.
❖ A glass containing a thin layer of salt.
❖ A dark mirror (magick mirror or black mirror).

Physical preparations...

Because you'll be using pure white aether to stir the winds, your mind needs to be pure, still, and very much at rest. Do this by any means that works for you, such as concentrating on the Divine Prayer (see page 1), or by using any other meditation technique until you are calm and able to focus completely on the ritual.

Magickal preparations...

Cast the magick circle (see page 73), making sure that you have all the necessary tools and magickal ingredients with you inside the circle. You may use any alternative circle casting if you so desire, or you may choose to perform the ritual under an alternative form of protection (such as an amulet, a protective spell, or a protected place).

Ritual instructions...

As soon the circle (or other protection) is complete, immediately light the ritual candle and allow a single drop of its wax to fall on the paper tag (which you have attached to the tied feathers) to form a permanent physical association between the candle and the intended weather pattern. As you make this wax bond, utter:

> Fire, Water, Earth, and Air,
> For magick gather here this day:
> Thought and purpose bonded strong,
> By wax this magick has its way.

Take up your athame and breathe fire, water, earth, and air energies from your body into the athame. Touch the tip of the athame to the tied feathers and allow the energy to be released in force, uttering:

> Elements of Fire and Earth,
> I call upon your counterpart,
> Elements of Air and Water,
> I summon thee by Ancient Art.
> Now zephyr stir and winds arise
> That stir the cloud across the skies.

Now breathe pure white aetheric energy from your body into the athame. Once again, touch the tip of the athame to the tied feathers and allow the energy to be released in force, uttering:

> *So mote it be!*

You may now break the magick circle (or leave your protective area) and ground yourself in order to keep your body energies balanced. A meal is highly recommended.

Final actions...

Keep the tied feathers somewhere safe until the magick has run its full course, or until the winds have served their purpose. Then strip the feathers, and either burn them or bury them, and the magick will cease functioning.

BANISHING WINDS

The intention...

To repel specific high winds from a specific location.

A word of warning: Every weather pattern has many effects. A high wind may be a nuisance in one spot, but it also moves other weather fronts along as it passes. When you reduce a high wind to a mere breeze, you may be stopping a spell of bad weather from moving on!

Equipment needed...

Specifically for this ritual, you will need the following items:

- ❖ A single feather.
- ❖ A paper tag (attached to the feather) on which you write the name or description of the location to be affected.
- ❖ A green candle (the Ritual Candle) mounted in a candleholder.

For the casting of a magick circle, you are going to need at the very least:

- ❖ Your athame or wand for casting the circle.
- ❖ A white candle in a candleholder (and matches, or a lighter).
- ❖ A glass containing some water.
- ❖ A glass containing a thin layer of salt.
- ❖ A dark mirror (magick mirror or black mirror).

Physical preparations...

Before you begin the ritual, clear your mind of any worries or unnecessary thoughts. If you allow unwanted thoughts or energies to interfere during the casting, your magick won't be as effective as it could have been.

Magickal preparations...

Cast the magick circle (see page 73), making sure that you have all the necessary tools and magickal ingredients with you inside the circle. You may use any alternative circle casting if you so desire, or you may choose to perform the ritual under an alternative form of protection (such as an amulet, a protective spell, or a protected place).

Ritual instructions...

As soon the circle (or other protection) is complete, immediately light the ritual candle and allow a single drop of its wax to fall on the feather to form a permanent physical association between the candle and the intended weather pattern. As you make this wax bond, utter:

> Fire, Water, Earth, and Air,
> For magick gather here this day:
> Thought and purpose bonded strong,
> By wax this magick has its way.

Take up your athame and breathe fire, water, earth, and air energies from your body into the athame. Touch the tip of the athame to the feather and allow the energy to be released in force, uttering:

> Fire, Earth, and Water true
> I speak unto your counterpart,
> Element of Air and winds,
> I banish thee by Ancient Art.
> Make calm and stillness soon prevail,
> The winds and breezes now to fail.

Now breathe pure white aetheric energy from your body into the athame. Once again, touch the tip of the athame to the feather and allow the energy to be released in force, uttering:

> So mote it be!

You may now break the magick circle (or leave your protective area) and ground yourself in order to keep your body energies balanced. A meal is highly recommended.

Final actions...
Immediately strip the feathers, and burn them or bury them to allow the magick to take effect.

ENCOURAGING NATURAL GROWTH

The intention...
To encourage the natural growth or regrowth of specific plant life.

Equipment needed...
For this ritual you will need the following items:
- ❖ Your athame.
- ❖ A green leaf, preferably of the same kind you want to have grow.
- ❖ A new cord of thirteen inches (32.5cm) in length (the Ritual Cord).

Physical preparations...
Before you begin the ritual you must be properly grounded, with your body's energies in harmony with the Earth's own energies. Try to make sure that you are in good health, and that you feel relaxed and centered — perhaps by repeating the Divine Prayer (see page 1) quietly to yourself.

You do not need to cast a magick circle unless you specifically wish to do so, or you have some reason to believe that you should. You may want to sit down at a table or on the ground for this ritual, because it may involve your becoming momentarily weary, dizzy, or disoriented.

Ritual instructions...
Take up your athame with both hands and hold the tip of it in front of your mouth. Visualize a stream of pure, elemental energy of Earth flowing from deep within you, up through your body and out through your mouth into the tip of the athame. Keep this up for as long as you can, stopping only when you begin to feel weary (sometimes you may feel dizzy as well).

Next, tie a knot in one end of the ritual cord, then wrap the cord around the stem of the athame and allow the earth energy to flow freely from the athame into the cord, uttering:

> *From nature's way this element flows;*
> *By nature's way this life now grows.*
> *From Earth to soil new life proceeds,*
> *May this new growth be free from weeds!*

Now take the cord and tie it securely around the green leaf, uttering:

> *So mote it be!*

It is very important that you now ground yourself in order to keep your body energies balanced. Take at least five or ten minutes to concentrate on absorbing earth-element energy from the environment around you; otherwise you'll end up with a headache and fatigue. You've given out a lot of your own earth energy, so you need to replenish it soon. After you've finished grounding and balancing yourself again, a meal is highly recommended.

Final actions...

As soon as you can, bury the cord (still tied around the green leaf) in the soil near the roots of the plants you wish to encourage. The cord will slowly leak its earth energy from the untied end, over time. As the green leaf decomposes, you'll see nature's full cycle of birth, growth, death, and decay, with the growing plants representing birth and growth, while the green leaf represents death and decay.

RETARDING NATURAL GROWTH

The intention...

To discourage the natural growth of specific unwanted plant life (weeds).

Equipment needed...

For this ritual you will need the following items:

- ❖ Your athame.
- ❖ A green stalk with at least one leaf, of the same species of plant you want to discourage (to be the witness of that plant life).
- ❖ A new cord of thirteen inches (32.5cm) in length (the Ritual Cord).

Physical preparations...

Clear your mind to allow yourself to focus on the subject (unwanted plant or plants). You don't need to cast a magick circle unless you specifically wish to do so, or you have a particular reason to believe that you need to.

Ritual instructions...

Place the witness (stalk and leaves) in front of you and touch the tip of your athame to the base of the stalk. Now visualize, for at least one minute, elemental earth energy being drawn from the stalk into the athame. Next, touch the athame's tip to the ground or to some unpopulated (barren) soil, uttering:

> From life to death this plant now goes,
> As all its Earth to Nature flows.

Once again touch the tip of your athame to the base of the stalk. Now visualize, for at least one minute, elemental water energy being drawn from the stalk into the athame. Next, touch the athame's tip to the ground or to some unpopulated (barren) soil, uttering:

> From life to death this plant now goes,
> As all its Water to Nature flows.

Once again touch the tip of your athame to the base of the stalk. Now visualize, for at least one minute, elemental air energy being drawn from the stalk into the athame. Next, touch the athame's tip to the ground or to some unpopulated (barren) soil, uttering:

> From life to death this plant now goes,
> As all its Air to Nature flows.

Once again touch the tip of your athame to the base of the stalk. Now visualize, for at least one minute, elemental fire energy being drawn from the stalk into the athame. Next, touch the athame's tip to the ground or to some unpopulated (barren) soil, uttering:

> From life to death this plant now goes,
> As all its Fire to Nature flows.

Tie a knot in one end of the ritual cord and place it next to the witness (stem and leaves). Touch the tip of your athame to the base of the stalk and visualize, for at least one minute, aetheric energy (the plant's life force) being drawn from the stalk into the athame. Next, touch the athame's tip to the untied end of the ritual cord and allow the plant's aetheric energy to flow completely into the cord, uttering:

> *From life to death this plant now goes,*
> *With life force bound, it will not grow.*

Quickly tie a knot at the remaining end of the ritual cord and utter:

> *So mote it be!*

You might want to ground yourself after handling the unwanted plant's energies. After you've finished grounding and balancing yourself again, a meal is highly recommended.

Final actions...

As soon as you can, bury the ritual cord in the soil next to, and preferably in contact with, the roots of the plant you wish to discourage. If a large area is to be treated, you may want to use a much longer cord, which you can bury surrounding the plants. Alternatively, you might choose to perform the ritual several times to create several such cords.

BANISHING INSOMNIA

The intention...

To help the sleepless get a good night's sleep.

Equipment needed...

Specifically for this ritual, you will need the following items:

❖ Any article (hair, photo, etc.) that is a witness of your subject (the magick's recipient).

❖ A new cord of thirteen inches (32.5cm) in length (the Ritual Cord).

❖ A white candle (the Ritual Candle) mounted in a candleholder.

For the casting of a magick circle, you are going to need at the very least:

❖ Your athame or wand for casting the circle.

❖ A white candle in a candleholder (and matches, or a lighter).

❖ A glass containing some water.

❖ A glass containing a thin layer of salt.

❖ A dark mirror (magick mirror or black mirror).

Physical preparations...

Make yourself conscious of the elements of Creation that surround you rather than dwelling on the troubles and unrest of everyday life. If you have any unresolved arguments or emotional disagreements with anyone, do your best to resolve them before starting this ritual. Also quiet your mind to ensure the smooth flow of magickal energies — perhaps by reciting the Divine Prayer (see page 1) until you feel calm and centered.

If there are several people to be treated, you will need to perform the ritual once for each of them, in every case using an appropriate witness and a new ritual cord.

Magickal preparations...

Cast the magick circle (see page 73), making sure that you have all the necessary tools and magickal ingredients with you inside the circle. You may use any alternative circle casting if you so desire, or you may choose to perform the ritual under an alternative form of protection (such as an amulet, a protective spell, or a protected place).

Ritual instructions...

As soon the circle (or other protection) is complete, immediately light the ritual candle and allow a single drop of its wax to fall on the witness to form a permanent physical association between the candle and the subject. For the same reason, dip each end of the ritual cord into the wax that melts beneath the ritual candle's flame (being careful not to set the cord alight). As you make these wax bonds, utter:

> *Fire, Water, Earth, and Air,*
> *Come gather now for magick pure:*
> *Cord and Witness bonded strong,*
> *By wax this magick will endure.*

Take up your athame and wrap the cord around it three times, taking hold of both ends with one hand and uttering:

> *In the name of all that is Divine,*
> *In the name of all Creation,*
> *And in the name of Love itself,*
> *I ask that* [state the name of your subject]
> *Will sleep in peace from this night forth.*
> *I ask you, strong and powerful God,*
> *That you will watch over* [his/her] *dreams.*

I ask you, fair and loving Goddess,
That you will quiet [his/her] mind at night.
In your wisdom, Divine One,
I ask for [his/her] restful slumber
From dusk until dawn.

Now breathe fire and air energies from your body into the athame and allow that energy to flow completely from the athame into the cord. Remove the cord and tie a single knot at one end, and then wind the cord back around the athame twice this time, uttering:

So mote it be.

Likewise, breathe water and earth energies from your body into the athame, and allow that energy to flow completely from the athame into the cord. Remove the cord and tie a single knot in the middle. Then wind the cord back around the athame just once this time, uttering:

So mote it be.

Finally, breathe pure white aetheric energy from your body into the athame and allow that energy to flow into the cord as well. Remove the cord and tie a single knot at the remaining end, uttering:

So mote it be.

Now extinguish the ritual candle. If you wish, you may now undertake any other magick that you want to perform while you are still magickally protected.

You may now break the magick circle (or leave your protective area) and ground yourself in order to keep your body energies balanced. A meal is highly recommended.

Final actions...
First of all, immediately go and burn or bury the witness. Now take the knotted cord and give it to the person or people who can't sleep and tell them to put it under their pillow somewhere near their head when they go to bed. Be sure to tell them not to untie the knots or to tie any more knots in the cord!

INDEX OF ARCANE SHADOWS

Finding employment
A ritual to help someone find the right job.

Blessing a place (home or otherwise)
A ritual to bless a place — home, office, garden, or any other site.

Summoning prosperity and success
A ritual to attract prosperity and success to a specific person's endeavors.

Protecting home and possessions
A ritual to protect a specific person's home and possessions from harm.

Banishing a problem
A ritual to banish a problem from your mind and from your life.

Imparting power to an object
A ritual to imbue a specific object with magickal energy, either as a charm or for energy storage.

Aetheric purification and balancing (grounding)
A ritual to aetherically purify yourself and ground yourself with Nature.

FINDING EMPLOYMENT

The intention...
To help someone find the right job. You can perform this ritual either for somebody else or for yourself.

Equipment needed...
- ❖ Any article (hair, photo, etc.) that is a witness of your subject (the magick's recipient). If the ritual is for yourself, you will still need a witness.
- ❖ A new cord of thirteen inches (32.5cm) in length (the Ritual Cord).
- ❖ A magnet of any type, the stronger the better (the Magickal Catalyst).
- ❖ Some coins, some dollars or banknotes, and a blank check, if possible (the Ritual Focus).
- ❖ A green candle and a red candle (the Ritual Candles) mounted in candleholders.

For the casting of a magick circle, you are going to need at the very least:
- ❖ Your athame or wand for casting the circle.

❖ A white candle in a candleholder (and matches, or a lighter).

❖ A glass containing some water.

❖ A glass containing a thin layer of salt.

❖ A dark mirror (magick mirror or black mirror).

Physical preparations...

Before you begin the ritual, clear your mind of the worries and concerns of life. Although it can be difficult to relax, I have found the Divine Prayer (see page 1) very useful in meditation.

Also, bear in mind that the money isn't there as the goal of the magick, but purely as a focus for your attention. Money is the end result of the real goal, which is getting the right job. Use the money to remind yourself of the goal of the magick.

Magickal preparations...

Cast the magick circle (see page 73), making sure that you have all the necessary tools and magickal ingredients with you inside the circle. You may use any alternative circle casting, if you so desire; or you may choose to perform the ritual under an alternative form of protection (such as an amulet, a protective spell, or a protected place).

Ritual instructions...

As soon the circle (or other protection) is complete, immediately light the ritual candles and allow a single drop of wax from each candle to fall on the witness to form a permanent physical association between the candles and the subject. For the same reason, dip each end of the ritual cord into the wax that melts beneath the ritual candle's flame (being careful not to set the cord alight). As you make these wax bonds, utter:

> Fire, Water, Earth, and Air,
> Come gather now for magick pure:
> Cord and Witness bonded strong,
> By wax this magick will endure.

Put your full attention on the Ritual Focus (the money) and allow your mind to see the subjects having a small amount of money available to them. Now slowly increase that fortune until you can envision them having earned lots of money in the new job. Envision them in work clothes, maybe carrying a briefcase or the tools of their trade. If they don't have a specific career or trade, then simply envision them arriving home after work, surrounded by all the good things that they could want. With that vision in mind, take up your athame and wrap the cord around it three times, taking hold of both ends with one hand and uttering:

> *In the name of all that is Divine,*
> *In the name of all Creation,*
> *And in the name of Truth and Honor,*
> *I proclaim that* [state the name of your subject]
> *Is now magickally linked with* [his/her] *next employer.*

Now touch the athame's tip to the magnet and utter:

> *I ask you, proud and powerful God,*
> *That* [his/her] *hunt for work will be shortened*
> *By the attraction of the work to worker.*
> *I ask you, fair and caring Goddess,*
> *That this willing worker will be fulfilled*
> *By the attraction of the worker to work.*
> *In your wisdom, Divine One,*
> *I ask for* [his/her] *employment happy and secure.*

Now breathe fire and air energies from your body into the athame, and allow that energy to flow completely from the athame into the cord. Remove the cord and tie a single knot at one end and then wind the cord back around the athame just twice this time, uttering:

> *So mote it be.*

Likewise, breathe water and earth energies from your body into the athame, and allow that energy to flow completely from the athame into the cord. Remove the cord and tie a single knot in the middle; then wind the cord back around the athame just once, uttering:

> *So mote it be.*

Finally, breathe pure white aetheric energy from your body into the athame, and allow that energy to flow into the cord as well. Remove the cord and tie a single knot at the remaining end, uttering:

> *So mote it be.*

Now extinguish the ritual candles. If you wish, you may at this point undertake any other magick that you want to perform while you are still magickally protected. You may now break the magick circle (or leave your protective area) and ground yourself in order to keep your body energies balanced. A meal is highly recommended.

Final actions...

Burn or bury the witness, and give the knotted cord to the people who need employment, telling them to keep it concealed somewhere about their person (perhaps in their briefcase or handbag) when they apply for jobs and go to interviews.

Be sure to tell them not to untie the knots until they have found, accepted, and started their new job.

The subject's part...

Now for the practical part: tell the subjects to apply for at least three different jobs every weekday until they are offered one that they can afford to accept. The magick can't force an employer to mysteriously pick up the phone and dial somebody they've never spoken to in order to offer them a job! What it will do, however, is give this person an advantage when applying for jobs — even getting them interviews where they may not otherwise have been given a chance. It will create a "magnetic" attraction between their personality and that of the potential employer, which will help in the interview. But the magick's recipient still has to dress right, have a good resume printed up, show a good attitude, and so on.

BLESSING A PLACE (HOME OR OTHERWISE)

The intention...

To bless a place — a home, office, garden, or any other site.

Equipment needed...

Specifically for this ritual you will need the following items:
- ❖ Your athame or wand.
- ❖ A white or light blue candle in a handheld candleholder (and matches, or a lighter).

Physical preparations...

If possible, take a walk around the building to familiarize yourself with the general layout. Devise a route that takes you through each distinct room or area. You may ask all other people present to leave before you begin, if you wish, or you may invite them to observe the ritual in silence. Note that you don't need to cast a magick circle or have any other form of magickal protection for a simple blessing ritual.

Ritual instructions...

Stand with your feet apart in the place where you propose to start your tour of the building, apartment, or garden, and hold your athame high above your head, pointing up toward the sky. Begin to slowly breathe in and out as deeply as you can. With each inhalation, envisage aetheric energy being drawn from the air into the athame, and all four elemental energies being drawn from the earth, up through your feet and legs, into your body. Do this for at least thirteen breaths. Afterwards, take a moment to compose yourself and return your breathing to normal while still holding the athame up high.

Now concentrate the elemental energies that you have accumulated and let them rise up your arms and out through your hands into your athame. Take a moment to allow your body to rebalance its elemental energies, then lower the athame. Light the ritual candle and use your athame to make the sign of the pentagram (five-pointed star) in the air, uttering:

> O Goddess, caring and loving,
> O God, strong and protective:
> Visit this place and keep it safe.
> Everywhere this candlelight flows,
> I ask you to watch over this place
> And bless it by grace and love divine.
> In all its days may this place be sacred,
> And may all within prosper and be happy.
> I ask you to bless this place with life,
> And with joy that comes from your love.
> Even in dark times, illuminate this place.
> Make certain the way within this place.
> I ask that your wisdom should prevail here.
> I ask out of true and honorable desire
> That this place should be a blessing to all.

Now move to each different room or area and make the sign of the pentagram using your athame. In each area, use the candle to illuminate all the
corners, nooks, and crannies. As you do, utter the opening enchantment:

> O Goddess, caring and loving,
> O God, strong and protective:
> Visit this place and keep it safe.
> Everywhere this candlelight flows,
> I ask you to watch over this place
> And bless it by grace and love divine.

When you have completed this in every room or area, go to the main entrance
— often the front door or a main gate. Here's a tip: It's easy to forget ponds,
gardens, sheds, garages, workshops, fields, or stables! You may also need an
enclosed candleholder or lamp if you're going to take the candle outside, to
keep it from blowing out in the breeze.

Now you need to release the unused energies from the athame back into the
earth, so touch the tip of your athame to the ground at the door or gateway,
and allow its energies to discharge completely into the ground. If you happen
to be blessing an apartment or an office that's not at ground level, you can still
do this, but you'll need to visualize the energy flowing down through the building back into the earth. When the energy has completely discharged, utter:

> O Goddess and God,
> I thank you for your attentions.
> I thank you for your blessings eternal.
> This place I leave in your trust and care.
> So mote it be!

Now extinguish the ritual candle. The ritual is complete, and it is now time
to have a drink and some food with your hosts; with any luck they will provide a meal for you!

SUMMONING PROSPERITY AND SUCCESS

The intention...

To attract prosperity and success to a specific person's endeavors.

Equipment needed...

Specifically for this ritual, you will need the following items:

❖ Any article (hair, photo, etc.) that is a witness of your subject (the magick's recipient).

❖ A new cord of thirteen inches (32.5cm) in length (the Ritual Cord).

❖ Some coins, some dollars or banknotes, and a blank check, if possible (the Ritual Focus).

❖ A green candle and a yellow or gold candle (the Ritual Candles) mounted in candleholders.

For the casting of a magick circle, you are going to need at the very least:

❖ Your athame or wand for casting the circle.

❖ A white candle in a candleholder (and matches, or a lighter).

❖ A glass containing some water.

❖ A glass containing a thin layer of salt.

❖ A dark mirror (magick mirror or black mirror).

Physical preparations...

Balance your energies well before starting this ritual. You can do this by grounding yourself (letting your body's energies harmonize with nature's forces), and by repeating the Divine Prayer (see page 1) until you feel calm and centered.

Magickal preparations...

Cast the magick circle (see page 73), making sure that you have all the necessary tools and magickal ingredients with you inside the circle. You may use any alternative circle casting, if you so desire; or you may choose to perform the ritual under an alternative form of protection (such as an amulet, a protective spell, or a protected place).

Ritual instructions...

As soon as the circle (or other protection) is complete, light the ritual candles and allow a single drop of wax from each candle to fall on the witness to form a permanent physical association between the candles and the subject. For the same reason, dip each end of the ritual cord into the wax that melts beneath the ritual candle's flame (being careful not to set the cord alight). As you make these wax bonds, utter:

> *Fire, Water, Earth, and Air,*
> *Come gather now for magick pure:*

> Cord and Witness bonded strong,
> By wax this magick will endure.

Focus your full attention on the Ritual Focus (the money), and allow your mind to see the subjects having plenty of money available to them. Now see them as being not only wealthy but happy, contented, and satisfied. Envision their satisfaction at being successful in all that they do. Bring to mind the feeling of satisfaction and success until it is almost your own. Now take up your athame and channel those feelings and images into it, uttering:

> To thee, forces of nature, I make this request,
> That [state the name of your subject] will know success
> And meet daily with health and wealth
> As long as [he/she] continues in honesty and truth,
> And in Generosity to the poor and those in need.
> I ask that you will grant [him/her] success
> In all that [he/she] undertakes for causes of goodness.
> By all that is Divine I make this request,
> On behalf of [state the name of your subject] this day.
> O Goddess of health and life,
> O God of prosperity and success,
> I thank you for your attentions!

Next, wrap the ritual cord three times around the athame and utter:

> In the name of all that is Divine,
> In the name of all Creation,
> And in the name of Truth and Honor,
> I proclaim that [state the subject's name], through this cord,
> Is now magickally linked with success and prosperity abundant.

Now breathe fire and air energies from your body into the athame. Allow that energy to flow completely from the athame into the cord. Remove the cord, and tie a single knot at one end. Then wind the cord back around the athame just twice this time, uttering:

> So mote it be.

Likewise, breathe water and earth energies from your body into the athame, and allow that energy to flow completely from the athame into the cord. Remove the cord and tie a single knot in the middle. Wind the cord back around the athame just once this time, uttering:

> So mote it be.

Finally, breathe pure white aetheric energy from your body into the athame and allow that energy to flow into the cord as well. Remove the cord and tie a single knot at the remaining end, uttering:

> *So mote it be.*

Now extinguish the ritual candles. If you wish, you may at this point undertake any other magick that you want to perform while you are still magickally protected.

You may now break the magick circle (or leave your protective area) and ground yourself in order to keep your body energies balanced. A meal is highly recommended.

Final actions...

First, go and burn or bury the witness in private. Next, give the knotted cord to your subjects, and instruct them to keep it concealed somewhere safe at home for a period of seven days, at which time they should untie just one of the knots. After that, they should notice some small change of fortune. After another seven days they must untie one more knot, leaving just one knot remaining in the cord. They should then see some change in the general direction of their life, toward a more successful or prosperous outlook. After another seven days they should untie the third and final knot and then burn or throw away the cord. Now the magick is complete and they should find themselves faced with a choice that will radically change their fortunes for the better — but offer them this warning: They must make the choice for themselves out of true and honest motives. Deceiving themselves or anybody else at that time will lead to misfortune and unhappiness for everyone involved.

On a note of ethics: success, prosperity, money, and power are not necessarily "evil." It's what you do with them that counts. It is up to you, as a responsible sorcerer, to cast this magick on those whom you sincerely believe are able to handle the resultant success. The magick calls on the Goddess and the God to supply prosperity to those who are true, honest, and generous of heart. Anyone who has abused that trust (judging from past experience) will probably prove unable to handle the consequences!

PROTECTING HOME AND POSSESSIONS

The intention...
To protect a specific person's home and possessions from harm.

Equipment needed...
Specifically for this ritual you will need the following items:
- ❖ Your athame or wand.
- ❖ A white or silver candle in a handheld candleholder (and matches, or a lighter).

Physical preparations...
Take a walk around the house or apartment to familiarize yourself with the general layout. Devise a route that takes you through each room, and through any access corridors, pathways, the driveway, garden, garage, and storage sheds. You may ask the owner and the rest of the family to leave before you begin, if you wish, or you may invite them to observe the ritual in silence. Note that you don't need to cast a magick circle or have any other form of magickal protection for a simple protection rite.

Ritual instructions...
Stand with your feet apart in the place where you propose to start your tour of the apartment or house (or garden), and hold your athame high above your head, pointing up toward the sky. Begin to slowly breathe in and out as deeply as you can. With each inhalation, envisage aetheric energy being drawn from the air into the athame, and all four elemental energies being drawn from the earth, up through your feet and legs, into your body. Do this for at least thirteen breaths. Afterwards, take a moment to compose yourself and return your breathing to normal while still holding the athame up high.

Now concentrate the elemental energies that you have accumulated and let them rise up your arms and out through your hands into your athame. Take a moment to allow your body to rebalance its elemental energies, then lower the athame. Light the ritual candle, and use your athame to make the sign of the pentagram (five-pointed star) in the air, uttering:

O Goddess, caring and loving,
O God, strong and protective:
Visit this place and keep it safe.
Everywhere this candlelight flows,
I ask you to watch over this place
And bless it by grace and love divine.
In all its days may this place be sacred,
And may all within prosper and be happy.
I ask you to bless this place with life,
And with joy that comes from your love.
Even in dark times, illuminate this place.
Make certain the way within this place.
I ask that your wisdom should prevail here.
I ask out of true and honorable desire
That this place should be a blessing to all.

Now move to each different room or area and make the sign of the pentagram using your athame. In each area, use the candle to illuminate all the
corners, nooks, and crannies. As you do so, utter the opening enchantment:

O Goddess, caring and loving,
O God, strong and protective:
Visit this place and keep it safe.
Everywhere this candlelight flows,
I ask you to watch over this place
And over its possessions which are dear,
And bless it by grace and love divine.

When you have completed this in every room (and in the garden, if they
have one), go to the main entrance — and open the front door or the front
gate. You may need to use an enclosed candleholder or lamp if you're going
to take the candle outside, to keep it from blowing out in the breeze.

Now you need to release the unused energies from the athame back into
the earth, so touch the tip of your athame to the ground at the door or gate,
and allow its energies to discharge completely into the earth. If you are
blessing an apartment that's not at ground level, you can still do this, but
you need to visualize the energy flowing down through the building back
into the earth. When the energy has completely discharged, utter:

O Goddess and God,
I thank you for your attentions.
I thank you for your blessings eternal.
This place I leave in your trust and care.
So mote it be!

Now extinguish the ritual candle. The ritual is complete. It is time to have a drink and some food with your hosts in their newly protected and blessed home.

BANISHING A PROBLEM

The intention...

To banish a problem from your mind and from your life.

One of the most useful of all the rituals, this is so general-purpose that it can help you with almost any problem you encounter. I have seen it being used to quickly cure headaches, migraines, back problems, colds, flu, and a number of other illnesses. You could use it to help you get over grief, anxiety, panic attacks, and everyday worries; or to rid your garden of unwanted insects or rodents. If you have a troublesome neighbor, or a quarrel with a friend or colleague, try using this ritual to clear up the problem. There's no end to the ways in which you can put it to use.

Equipment needed...

❖ The largest apple you can find.
❖ A sharp knife (for cutting up the apple).

Ritual instructions...

This is perhaps the simplest possible "bind and dispel" rite. Focus and concentrate your mind on the apple, then say aloud:

Apple pure, fruit of tree,
Take ye now this ache from me...

Now tell the apple, in as much or little detail as you like, the nature of your problem. For example, you might tell it that you're angry at a friend for saying something mean about you, or that your dog was killed by a car and you can't forgive the driver. Perhaps you're just worried about something that may or may not happen.

Take the knife and cut the apple into at least four pieces (or more if the problem is very intense — just take care not to develop negative feelings toward the apple itself!). Go outside and bury the pieces of apple together in the ground, where they can rot away and be returned to the earth, from whence they came. As the apple fades away into the earth, the unwanted problem or feelings will also fade away.

Final actions...
Don't ever dig up the apple again, even if it's only to see if it has rotted away yet. The whole point is that you've buried the problem and walked away.

IMPARTING POWER TO AN OBJECT

The intention...
To imbue a specific object with magickal energy, either as a charm or for energy storage.

Equipment needed...
Specifically for this ritual, you will need the following items:
- Any objects that are to be empowered (you can empower as many as you like in one ritual session).
- A white or purple candle (the Ritual Candle) mounted in a suitable candleholder.

For the casting of a magick circle, you are going to need at the very least:
- Your athame or wand for casting the circle.
- A white candle in a candleholder (and matches, or a lighter).
- A glass containing some water.
- A glass containing a thin layer of salt.
- A dark mirror (magick mirror or black mirror).

Physical preparations...
Make sure you are free of unwanted thoughts and energies before you begin the ritual. If anything is troubling your mind when you perform this ritual, the aetheric pattern of your troubled thoughts may also be imprinted in the object — giving the object a "troubled" energy field. Try concentrating on

the Divine Prayer (see page 1), repeating it quietly over and over, until you feel ready to proceed.

Magickal preparations...

Cast the magick circle (see page 73), making sure that you have all the necessary tools and magickal ingredients with you inside the circle. This ritual depends heavily upon the casting of the magick circle, so you will need to do that even if you are already operating under some other form of magickal protection.

Ritual instructions...

Light the ritual candle. Stand in the middle of the circle, facing North. Turn around sunwise three times, pausing at East, South, West, and North to bow to each direction (each element). When you reach North for the third time, sit down.

Pick up an object that is to be empowered and focus your mind on it. First, you need to assign a unique magickal name to the object (to give it an identity of its own). Second, you need to tell the object what its lifetime is (how long it will last before its power expires). It is very important to physically tell the object these things, so there is no doubt. As pointed out previously, lifetime should always be whatever length of time the object is needed, or until your own death, whichever comes sooner (in this way you ensure that your magick dies with you). After you have told the object who it is and how long it must live, utter:

> Thou of the elements
> Who know my wish,
> To empower this article
> For the magickal service
> Of its creator, grant it now.

If you have a specific magickal purpose in mind for the object, such as making it a "safe travel" talisman, now describe the purpose of the object, or cast any enchantment necessary before putting the object down again.

If there are other objects to be empowered, follow the same procedure for each in turn (name the object, give it a lifetime, ask the elements to empower it, and tell the object its purpose, if appropriate).

When you have finished empowering the objects, stand up and bow to each quarter three times as before. Finally, sit down and utter:

My many thanks,
Thou of the elements,
For thy aid.

The rite is done. Extinguish the ritual candle. If you wish, you may now undertake any other magick that you want to perform while you are still magickally protected. You may then break the magick circle and ground yourself in order to keep your body energies balanced. A meal is highly recommended.

AETHERIC PURIFICATION AND BALANCING (GROUNDING)

The intention...
To aetherically purify yourself and ground yourself with nature.

Equipment needed...
❖ A clean patch of ground to sit on. Alternatively, a seat of any kind will do.
❖ A tree or wall to prop yourself up against (as a support, in case you feel dizzy or tired).

Physical preparations...
Loosen any tight clothing and make sure that you are in an environment where you are not likely to be interrupted or distracted by anyone or anything. Although the ideal circumstances are a quiet, natural, and uncluttered place, this rite can still be safely carried out even in a car in a parking lot.

Ritual instructions...
Sit outdoors, if possible, in a comfortable position, with your feet in contact with the ground. It may help to prop yourself up against a tree or a wall. Clear your mind of all the worries of the day, and concentrate on the Divine Prayer (see page 1) until you feel basically calm at heart.

Now loosely clasp your hands together, with your fingers interlocked and your palms facing or even touching each other. Keep both feet firmly on the ground or, if you are indoors, on the floor. It would be best if your feet were in physical contact with the earth itself, but if there are other things (including other floors of the building) in the way, then you simply have to "see past it" in your mind as you carry out this rite.

It is a good idea to keep your eyes closed in the next stages, to avoid the risk of visual distractions.

In your mind, picture your body drawing a luxurious mix of elemental energies up from the Earth, through your feet and legs. Now picture your arms drawing purest white aetheric energy from the atmosphere around and above you. Keep these flows of energy going until you start to feel light-headed or dizzy (it may take anything from a few seconds to a few minutes). This is the point at which your body has absorbed all the energies it can and is highly charged with all five elements.

Now you need to balance the energies and let them even themselves out in harmony with nature and the Earth. Start to slowly breathe in and out as deeply as you can — but only thirteen times in total, no more, no less. As you breathe in, visualize your body's excess energies being pushed to the palms of your hands and the soles of your feet. As you breathe out, visualize that energy being dispersed back into the Earth and the atmosphere around you. When all thirteen deep breaths are done, sit in silence for as long as you need in order to settle your mind again before opening your eyes.

Final actions...

An optional extra that helps to build a positive attitude and outlook to the day: just before opening your eyes at the end of the balancing rite, think of one thing from the last 24 hours that pleases you, or alternatively think about a new positive attitude that you want to develop. As your mind and body enter a restful state, your first thoughts are of good, pleasing, and positive matters. This is a good step toward programming yourself for an even more relaxed and positive outlook.

9 CHAPTER

GRIMOIRE OF ENCHANTMENT MAGICK

Where did this grimoire come from?

The enchantments (spells) in this grimoire of magick have been brought together from the Book of Shadows and Enchantments of the Beneviche Order of Sorcery. As you read and use them, you may want to change the words, visualizations, and preparations to suit the way you like to work. Particularly when casting a spell "on the spot," you'll find that there isn't always the time (or opportunity) to prepare fully — in which case you'll need to adapt your spell as you go. Although that isn't the ideal situation, you'll find that all the spells are well structured enough to make that job easy.

You'll find that most of the spells have been written up to be cast for other people. If you want to cast them for yourself, and there are no specific instructions about that, treat yourself in the same way you would treat any other subject. If you need a witness (such as a photograph), then use a photograph of yourself. And when the words to be spoken refer to the subject, just say "me" or your own name instead.

May your works be successful and your days in the Craft be long and fruitful. Blessed be!

INDEX OF SMALL ENCHANTMENTS

Casting emotional strength
A spell to emotionally strengthen a specific person for a limited time.

Casting physical strength
A spell to physically strengthen a specific person for a limited time.

Casting mental clarity
A spell to bring mental clarity to a specific person, about a specific subject.

Casting mental confusion
A spell to bring mental confusion about a specific subject to a specific person for a limited time.

Casting persuasion
A spell to enable you to persuade a specific person about a specific subject.

Casting an emotional sedative
A spell to emotionally sedate a specific person for a limited time.

Releasing a headache
A spell to relieve most headaches induced by stress, food, or drink.

Charming an animal
A spell to charm an animal into a passive mood or into submission.

BLESSING FOR SAFE TRAVEL

The intention...
To protect travelers from harm as they journey from place to place.

Physical preparations...
When you cast this spell, you need to be able to touch, see, or hear each person to whom the spell applies, or be able to touch an article (hair, photo, etc.) that is a witness of each person to be affected. If your psychic abilities are very strong, you will be able to cast the spell by forming a psychic bond with them (whether or not they reciprocate that bond).

Your mind needs to be quite relaxed and calm before you begin. Try visualizing yourself as a calm ocean, forceful and active but still at peace within itself. Or perhaps repeat the Divine Prayer (see page 1) over and over until you feel ready.

Magickal preparations...

Ideally, this spell should be cast on the Wednesday before the travel is due to begin, due to the day's association with Mercury and travel. If the moon is in a waning cycle at the time of casting, concentrate on the reduction of the dangers and perils of travel. If the moon is in a waxing cycle at the time of casting, concentrate on the physical and spiritual protection of the traveler.

The enchantment...

Utter the verse aloud, once for each person to whom the magick is to apply, concentrating on either their image or the sound of their voice (both of which are normally quite unique, so either should be sufficient to identify your subject).

> Be thou protected in rest and motion,
> Be thou rested in thy travels.
> When light dawns early,
> And when darkness draws near,
> May thy journey be safe and secure.
> Thy mind and body safe shall be,
> For God and Goddess go with thee.
> May thou travel in Holy safety
> Until thy journey's end.

With the index finger of your right hand, draw the sign of the pentagram in the air in front of you to seal the spell, uttering:

> So mote it be.

The spell is complete.

Final actions...

Bid each traveler a safe journey and a timely return (if they're returning, that is!). If your budget allows, give each traveler a pentagram charm or pendant as a reminder of the spell of protection that has been sealed.

FINDING THE RIGHT PLACE TO BE

The intention...
To help someone find the right house, apartment, or office.

Physical preparations...
You need to know three things before you can cast this simple spell: the name of the subject, the name of the town or area where they'd like to find a place, and an idea of how soon they would be ready to move in.

Before you begin, find a quiet place to relax. If you're casting the spell for yourself, imagine yourself walking quietly through the ideal place. Picture every detail, the size of every room, the surroundings outside. If you cast the spell for somebody else, try your best to imagine their ideal surroundings.

Magickal preparations...
If possible, cast the spell on a Wednesday because of the day's associations with time, money, efficiency, and movement. A trouble-free move to an affordable place should then be possible within a short time! If the moon is in a waxing phase, concentrate on finding the right place. If the moon is in a waning phase, concentrate instead on needing to move on from an existing place.

The enchantment...
Utter the verse aloud:

> Goddess of all, who is fair and kind,
> I ask you now this spell to bind:
> That [your subject's name] should find
> Your clear and certain sign
> Of what is sure and what is right.
> I beseech you now to hear this, my request...

At this point, describe (in as much detail as possible) the kind of office, house, or apartment that is wanted. Name the desired town or area, describe the size and value of the property that is needed, and specify the date by which the subject wants to move in. Be as specific as you can — the more information you can give, the better. If possible, stop for a few moments and concentrate on your mental walk-through of that place. Then continue with the verse:

In times like this, I seek your Grace.
In days to come, make known the place.
The moon shall wax, the future starts,
The moon shall wane, the past departs.
To [him/her] the place must soon be shown;
In wisdom and authority, make it so!

With the index finger of your right hand, draw the sign of the pentagram in the air in front of you to seal the spell, uttering:

So mote it be.

The spell is complete.

Final actions...
Suggest to your subjects that they immediately start looking for appropriate places, checking property listings for the area in which they're interested. They will start seeing suitable houses, apartments, or offices within a matter of a few days, and, when they visit the right one, they will instinctively know that it is the right place for them to be.

CASTING EMOTIONAL STRENGTH

The intention...
To emotionally strengthen a specific person for a limited time.

Physical preparations...
You need to be able to touch, see, or hear each person to whom the spell applies, or be able to touch an article (hair, photo, etc.) that is a witness of each person to be affected. If your psychic abilities are very strong, you will be able to cast the spell by forming a psychic bond with the subject.

Your body should be in good physical health, and your mind clear and calm before you cast this spell. I find the Divine Prayer is very effective as a focus for my attention while I ground myself with nature's energies. The Divine Prayer can be found on page 1 of this book.

Magickal preparations...

Ideally, this spell should be cast on a Monday, due to the day's association with the moon and with human emotions and feelings. If the moon is in a waning cycle at the time of casting, concentrate on the reduction of unwanted emotional states. If the moon is waxing at the time of casting, concentrate on strengthening the subject's state of mind and emotional well-being.

The enchantment...

Utter the verse aloud, concentrating on either the subject's image or the sound of his/her voice. If circumstances and location allow, it is best if you can place the palm of your left hand flat on the top of the recipient's head.

> The moon does wax and wane in seasons
> And so controls emotion's reasons.
> As moon does wax, increase your strength;
> As moon does wane, decrease your weakness.
> Self control and justice too
> Must now prevail in all you do.
> Control and strength in the high and the low,
> By Nature's order, make it so!

With the index finger of your right hand, draw the sign of the pentagram in the air in front of you to seal the spell, uttering:

> So mote it be.

The spell is complete.

Final actions...

Make sure your subjects know that their newfound emotional strength is there only until the next new moon. Depending upon which part of the 28-day cycle the moon is in, the spell will last for up to 28 days.

It's also important to make your subjects understand that they won't be unaffected by emotional events or scenes. Quite the opposite — they might become extremely emotional under some circumstances, but they will be able to control themselves and not allow emotion to overcome their better judgment.

CASTING PHYSICAL STRENGTH

The intention...
To physically strengthen a specific person for a limited time.

Physical preparations...
You need to be able to touch, see, or hear each person to whom the spell applies, or be able to touch an article (hair, photo, etc.) that is a witness of each person to be affected. If your psychic abilities are very strong, you will be able to cast this spell by forming a psychic bond with them.

Magickal preparations...
Ideally, this spell should be cast on a Thursday, due to the day's association with Jupiter and with power, strength, and success. If the moon is in a waning cycle at the time of casting, concentrate on the reduction of weaknesses in muscle tissues. If the moon is in a waxing cycle, concentrate on strengthening the subject's muscles and physical coordination.

The enchantment...
Utter the verse aloud, concentrating on either your subjects' image or the sound of their voice. If circumstances and location allow, it is best if you can place the palm of your left hand flat on the top of the recipients' head. Or, if the spell is meant to apply to a specific muscle or group of muscles, touch that area of their body, if appropriate.

> *Your strength is in your body already,*
> *As Jupiter arcs its orbit true.*
> *Your strength is linked with Jupiter's power,*
> *And Jupiter's force is linked with you.*
> *The moon does wax and wane in time*
> *And so your strength with it will climb.*
> *As moon does wax, increase your strength;*
> *As moon does wane, decrease your weakness.*
> *Control and power, with justice too*
> *Must now prevail in all you do.*
> *Energy and reflex for action grow,*
> *By Nature's order, make it so!*

With the index finger of your right hand, draw the sign of the pentagram in the air in front of you to seal the spell, uttering:

> So mote it be.

The spell is complete.

Final actions...

Let the spell's recipients know that their newfound physical strength is only a very temporary measure: It will be at its peak at the next full moon, and it will cease completely at the next new moon. They won't be able to use strength that their body doesn't already have. The spell won't enable them to lift weights that their body frame can't support, nor will it allow them to run faster than their legs can actually carry them! It will, however, enable them to use their muscles and body energy more efficiently than usual, bringing them to their own peak of physical ability. This spell also has a commonly observed side effect: reflexes and coordination seem to improve in many cases, along with strength. In short, the sluggish and the weary often become the rapid and the energetic.

CASTING MENTAL CLARITY

The intention...

To bring mental clarity to a specific person, about a specific subject.

Physical preparations...

When you cast this spell, you need to be able to touch, see, or hear each person to whom the spell applies, or be able to touch an article (hair, photo, etc.) that is a witness of each person to be affected.

If your mind is not calm and centered, visualize a peaceful place — maybe a green pasture with a gentle stream flowing through it — and focus your attention on the tranquility and restfulness that surrounds you. Alternatively, you might say the Divine Prayer quietly to yourself (see page 1).

Magickal preparations...

Ideally, this spell should be cast on a Sunday, due to the day's association with the sun and with logic, thought, and enlightenment. If the moon is in a waning cycle at the time of casting, concentrate on reducing confusion in the subjects' mind. If the moon is in a waxing cycle, concentrate on increasing the subjects' cognitive abilities and the clarification of their thoughts.

The enchantment...

Utter the verse aloud, concentrating on either your subjects' image or the sound of their voice. If circumstances and location allow, it is best if you can place the palm of your left hand flat on the top of the recipients' head.

> *In the mind's confusion danger lies;*
> *The Sun brings clarity through the skies.*
> *As daybreak comes your thoughts are clear.*
> *As evening falls your thoughts are clear.*
> *While you sleep your thoughts relax.*
> *Clarity joins your thoughts together,*
> *Which then confusion cannot sever.*
> *As the moon does wax and wane in time*
> *So your clarity with it will climb.*
> *As moon does wax, your mind is strong;*
> *As moon does wane, confusion has gone.*
> *Self control and justice too*
> *Must now prevail in all you do.*
> *Calm clear thoughts in the high and the low,*
> *By Nature's order, make it so!*

With the index finger of your right hand, draw the sign of the pentagram in the air in front of you to seal the spell, uttering:

> *So mote it be.*

The spell is complete.

Final actions...

Tell the recipients that their increased mental clarity will last only as long as the current moon (until the next new moon begins). The spell won't increase their IQ, nor will it give them access to knowledge or wisdom that they don't already have at their command. It will, however, enable them to think more quickly, clearly, logically, and accurately than usual. In most cases, coordination and spatial judgment are also likely to be improved.

CASTING MENTAL CONFUSION

The intention...

To bring mental confusion about a specific subject to a specific person for a limited time.

A word of warning: There are very few circumstances under which you should ever have need of this spell, because, unless you have direct permission from the recipient of the spell (and that doesn't seem likely), it breaks the Sorcerer's Code. The most likely use for this spell is when somebody needs to be genuinely confused — when they don't want to reveal a secret by mistake, or give away information that must be kept private. You might also choose (at your own risk) to apply the spell to someone who is threatening the lives of others.

Physical preparations...

You'll need to be able to touch, see, or hear each person to whom the spell applies, or be able to touch something that acts as a witness of each person. If your psychic abilities are strong, you can cast the spell by forming a psychic bond with them.

Your mind should be relaxed and calm before you begin, otherwise you run the risk of the magick's affecting you as well. Quietly recite the Divine Prayer (see page 1) until you feel you can focus sufficiently on the magick.

Magickal preparations...

Ideally, this spell should be cast on a Saturday, due to the day's association with Saturn and with limitations, boundaries, slowness, and understanding. If the moon is in a waning cycle at the time of casting, concentrate on reducing the subject's cognitive efficiency. If the moon is in a waxing cycle at the time of casting, concentrate on encouraging the subject's mind to slow down and to find mental barriers at every turn.

The enchantment...

Concentrate either on the subjects' image or the sound of their voice. If circumstances and location allow, it is best if you can either point at the recipients with your left index finger, or place the palm of your left hand flat on the top of the recipients' head. Keeping in mind your aim (the area of thought that is to be confused), repeat this first chant either in your mind or aloud, envisaging a fog of confusion filling the subjects' mind:

> Confusion, uncertainty, a fog of the mind,
> This spell, while I wish it, your clarity bind.

When the fog is complete, repeat this chant in the same way, this time envisaging the spell charging the fog you've already created in their mind:

> By Saturn and darkness and dreaming combined,
> The things I would hide will be hid from your mind.

With the index finger of your right hand, draw the sign of the pentagram in the air in front of you to seal the spell, uttering:

> So mote it be.

The spell is complete.

Final actions...

Take any measures that you consider appropriate to ensure the safety of the recipients (and anyone for whom they are responsible) during the period of the spell's effect. Should you need to cancel the spell quickly, use the "Dispelling Unwanted Magick" arcane enchantment (see page 181). Note that the spell is effective until you cancel it, or until the next new moon (whichever comes first), but please note: it is considered highly irresponsible to let this spell run for more than a few hours.

CASTING PERSUASION

The intention...

To enable you to persuade a specific person about a specific subject.

A word of warning: There are very few circumstances under which you should ever have need of this spell, because (unless you have permission from the recipient of the spell) it breaks the Sorcerer's Code. The most obvious occasion that legitimately calls for this spell is when you are faced with someone who is threatening lives. The ability to persuade such a person to stand down is welcome in such situations.

Physical preparations...

When you cast this spell, you need to be able to touch, see, or hear each person to whom the spell applies, or be able to touch something that represents them.

Your body should ideally be in good health before you cast this spell. Relax and calm your mind, as total clarity of thought is required. If you need to ground and balance yourself, try visualizing a perfectly cut diamond, with light glinting from every facet. Diamonds represent purity of spirit and thought alike.

Magickal preparations...

Ideally, this spell should be cast on a Thursday, due to the day's association with Jupiter and with human charisma and power. If the moon is in a waning cycle at the time of casting, concentrate on reducing the subject's desire to disagree or to think for themselves. If the moon is in a waxing cycle at the time of casting, concentrate on increasing the subject's desire to be persuaded or to conform.

The enchantment...

Look straight into the subjects' eyes, or touch their hand or shoulder with yours, and form the spell using only thought, not spoken words! You will need to practice this spell by looking into your own eyes in the mirror until you become confident and quick enough to be able to cast the spell without causing suspicion. The simple mind chant is this:

> Do my Will;
> Agree with all I say,
> By Jupiter's force I'll have my way.

You will need to use your psychic intuition to determine when (if at all) the magick's recipients are susceptible to your suggestions. You may need to repeat the chant in your mind more than once before they reach that point. When that point is reached, disengage your visual or hand-to-shoulder contact and carry on making your point as normal. If the spell has worked, they will find themselves in general agreement with you.

Final actions...

It is completely up to you whether or not you ever let the recipients know that they have been enchanted in this way. Remember, though, that forcing others to think, say, or do things without their knowledge and permission is considered black magick, because it breaks the Sorcerer's Code.

CASTING AN EMOTIONAL SEDATIVE

The intention...

To emotionally sedate a specific person for a limited time. This should be done only when the recipient is in an overemotional state and isn't responding to more traditional and practical calming techniques (such as sitting down, relaxing the body, sleeping, drinking herbal teas, and so on).

Physical preparations...

You need to be able to touch, see, or hear each person to whom the spell applies, or be able to touch an article that is a witness of each person to be affected (such as a lock of hair, or a recent photograph).

Relax and calm your mind before you begin casting the spell, and ground your body's energies thoroughly, otherwise you may end up being affected by the magick yourself!

Magickal preparations...

Ideally, this spell should be cast on a Monday, due to the day's association with the moon and with human emotions and feelings. If the moon is in a waning cycle at the time of casting, concentrate on reducing the subjects' emotional turmoil and unwanted thoughts. If the moon is in a waxing cycle at the time of casting, concentrate on feeding their mind's desire for emotional calm and stability.

The enchantment...

If circumstances and location allow, get recipients of the spell to lie down, close their eyes, and relax their body as much as possible. It is best if you can place the palm of your left hand flat on the top of the recipients' head. At the very least, you should be in the same room or area as the spell's recipients (so that they can hear you speak). Now loudly and clearly speak out the verse:

> Emotion's turmoil has no real power;
> The Moon brings peace with every hour.
> As daybreak comes, your feelings fade.
> As evening falls, emotions wane.
> While you sleep your thoughts relax.
> Calmness joins your thoughts together,

Which then emotion cannot sever.
As the Moon does wax and wane in time
So the harmony with it will climb.
As Moon does wax, your mind is strong;
As Moon does wane, turmoil is gone.
Calmest feelings in the high and the low,
By Nature's order, make it so!

With the index finger of your right hand, draw the sign of the pentagram in the air in front of you to seal the spell, uttering:

So mote it be.

The spell is complete.

Final actions...

Write out the words of the verse on a piece of paper or card. Also on the card, record the date on which the spell was cast and the date of the next new moon (that is, the spell's expiration date). Fold it over and seal it in an envelope and give it to the recipients of the spell, telling them to open and read it in one or two day's time. After the new moon, you will need to cast the spell again, if they desire.

RELEASING A HEADACHE

The intention...

To relieve most headaches induced by stress, food, or drink.

You can also use this spell to help the symptoms of a hangover (but it won't prevent alcohol from damaging your body in other ways). Migraines can also be relieved greatly, but you need to seek medical advice as well.

Physical preparations...

Although this spell was originally intended for self-healing, it can be adapted for use on other people by altering the wording slightly in any places you think appropriate. If you choose to cast the spell for others, you should be in good physical health yourself before proceeding.

Your mind needs to be quite relaxed and calm before you begin. If it is not already peaceful, try visualizing yourself as a calm ocean, forceful and active but still at peace within itself. It sometimes helps to visualize yourself in a thick fog that, as you relax, slowly lifts until you can see clearly around you. You can also try repeating the Divine Prayer (see page 1) quietly, until you feel ready to continue.

Magickal preparations...
Ideally, this spell should be cast on a Saturday, due to the day's association with Saturn and with sickness and health, limitations, disability, and stoppages. If the moon is in a waning cycle at the time of casting, concentrate on reducing the cause and symptoms of the headache. If the moon is in a waxing cycle, concentrate on increasing the body's ability to fight off the headache.

The enchantment...
Clear your mind of all thoughts, images, and worries of the day. Concentrate deeply on that inner darkness and imagine the black void being filled completely with a comforting warmth. Touch the palm of your right hand to your head in the place where the pain feels worst, or to the crown of your head. Now simply command your body to respond to the warmth of that clear space in your mind, uttering:

> Of Aether forged, the calm clear mind
> Commands the body in harmony to bind.
> As thoughts of peace and stillness flow
> I command this headache now to go.
> Deep inside the healing fires burn,
> I command this headache to not return.

With the index finger of your right hand, draw the sign of the pentagram in the air in front of you to seal the spell, uttering:

> So mote it be.

The spell is complete.

Final actions...
Lie down somewhere quiet where you can be undisturbed for five or ten minutes. Close your eyes, but try not to fall asleep unless you have plenty of

time to spare. Now relax each muscle in your body, working from your feet up to your head. When you have relaxed your body, just lie still and clear your mind of all thoughts. If any thoughts come to mind during this time, tell them to go away and cast them out of your mind, concentrating on that clear and warm darkness in your mind's eye. The headache will go away in a few minutes (or sometimes less) and not return. By the way, always get up slowly after any relaxation exercise, otherwise, you may feel dizzy!

CHARMING AN ANIMAL

The intention...
To charm an animal into a passive mood or into submission.

Physical preparations...
When you cast this spell, you need to be able to touch, see, or hear each animal to whom the spell applies. This is a psychic spell and will require you to have acquired excellent psychic and telepathic abilities. Psychic bonding with animals can be a very disturbing experience, as you may encounter animal reflexes and thought patterns that are quite different from those of fellow human beings!

Your mind needs to be quite relaxed and calm before you begin. If you don't have time to calm your mind, it would be a good idea to recite the Divine Prayer aloud (see page 1). If you have the luxury of time, it may be useful to use meditation or positive visualization techniques to ground and balance yourself. Use this opportunity to restore your body's natural balance of energies before trying to interact with animals.

Magickal preparations...
Although it may be necessary to cast this spell at a moment's notice, it will work best if cast on a Thursday, due to the day's association with Jupiter and with human charisma, leadership, and power. If the moon is in a waning cycle at the time of casting, concentrate on reducing the animal's own will-power. If the moon is in a waxing cycle, concentrate on creating a desire, within the animal's mind, to cooperate with you under all circumstances.

The enchantment...
You need to look into the animal's eyes, point your right index finger at the

animal, and touch it, or you need to form a psychic bond with the animal. Once you have established that link, clear your mind and visualize yourself in the form of the animal. For example, if the animal is a bulldog, visualize your spirit taking on the shape and appearance of a bulldog of the same size and appearance. This helps the animal to recognize you as an equal, and, because their eyes and psychic senses are giving them conflicting information about what you really are, they will be confused enough to allow a psychic bond to take hold. Once you feel that you have established both equality and communication, hum a low-pitched note aloud from your throat and repeat this chant as many times as necessary in your mind:

> *I will not harm you, and you will not harm me.*
> *I require your cooperation; this is nature's way.*
> *I am from a higher realm; recognize me and obey.*

You will need to use your psychic intuition to determine when the animal is susceptible to your suggestions. You may need to repeat the chant in your mind more than once before it reaches that point.

Final actions...

Once the spell has been cast, it will last only while you are in the animal's presence. As soon as you are out of sight, the animal no longer has your spirit image as the frame of reference that was making you its equal. Most animals will not pursue you after the spell has been broken, but always be prepared for such an eventuality.

If you need to communicate any other specific instructions, requests, or commands to the animal while it is still under your influence, do so by simple psychic telepathy. Remember to keep your spirit image looking like the animal when you communicate; otherwise, the animal will probably reject your thoughts and commands.

INDEX OF ARCANE ENCHANTMENTS

Blessing food and drink
A spell to bless food and drink before it is consumed.

Banishing bodily pain
A spell to banish bodily aches and pains for yourself, other people, or even animals.

Heightening intuition
A spell to heighten a specific person's mental and psychic intuition.

Manifesting an image (illusion)
A spell to cause an image to appear temporarily, or to alter the physical appearance temporarily.

Forming an aethereal shield
A spell to form an aethereal shield of protection around a specific person, object, or area.

Dispelling unwanted magick
A spell to dispel the power of any unwanted magick that you suspect may be at work within a specific area, including magickally created illusions.

BLESSING FOOD AND DRINK

The intention...
To bless and cleanse food and drink before it is consumed.

Physical preparations...
Relax, calm your mind, and get rid of all unnecessary thoughts and worries. Make sure you're comfortable, and in a place where you won't be interrupted. Your mind needs to be quite relaxed and calm before you begin. Try repeating the Divine Prayer (see page 1) quietly until you feel calm and trouble-free enough to proceed.

Magickal preparations...
This spell obviously may need to be cast on any day of the week, yet will surely function most efficiently on a Sunday, due to the day's association with the sun and with life and spiritual matters. If the moon is in a waning

cycle at the time of casting, concentrate on negating any negative or harmful energies in the food and drink. If the moon is in a waxing cycle, concentrate on creating a harmony of energies within the food and drink.

The enchantment...

This enchantment needs to be committed to memory, and it is always a good thing if everybody present joins in saying the verse.

Hold your hands out over the food and drink, palms facing downward. Visualize any harmful energies in the food being released and sent away as you utter:

> *Goddess pure and God of power,*
> *Bless this food and drink this hour.*
> *We ask for health and benefit*
> *From nutrients we gain from it.*
> *We thank you.*
> *We praise you.*
> *We thank you.*

The blessing and cleansing is complete, and the food and drink should be consumed immediately.

BANISHING BODILY PAIN

The intention...

To banish bodily aches and pains for yourself, other people, or even animals.

Because this spell can be so useful for self-healing and also for helping others (even animals) who are in pain, I have provided two sets of instructions: one for yourself, and one for banishing the pain of others.

Physical preparations...

If you are banishing your own pain, find a quiet place where you can relax without being interrupted. Take the phone off the hook, lock the doors, close the windows, turn off the television, and lie down somewhere comfortable, flat on your back with your arms down by your sides. Allow your body to slowly relax as much as possible.

No matter who the subject is (whether it is you or someone else), take a moment or two to ground yourself and allow your body's energies to balance themselves and harmonize with nature's energies. If your mind is full of worries or thoughts, try to dismiss them. If you need to clear your mind, try reciting the Divine Prayer to yourself over and over (see page 1).

Magickal preparations...

Although you might have to cast this spell on any day of the week, it will work best on a Saturday, because of the day's association with matters of sickness and health. When the moon is in its waning cycle, concentrate on reducing the pain that is felt. If the moon is in its waxing cycle, concentrate instead on strengthening the body's defenses against the cause of the pain.

The enchantment...

The verse of the enchantment is very short, so it can be memorized easily — and you can use it no matter where you are. One point to remember is that although the words of the spell are normally spoken aloud, the spell can also work if you simply "think it into being." In that case, your level of psychic ability will determine how effective the results are.

For banishing your own pains: concentrate on the specific area of your body that needs pain relief, and repeat this verse seven times:

> Goddess Hecate, wizened crone,
> Let your healing here be done.
> This body heal, its pain decrease,
> To cure the cause, your power release!

When banishing pain for others: concentrate on the specific part of their body that needs pain relief and, if they can possibly participate, ask them to do the same. You can also adapt the verse for animals by replacing the word "person" with "creature." Repeat this verse aloud seven times:

> Goddess Hecate, wizened crone,
> Let your healing here be done.
> This [person/creature] heal, their pain decrease,
> To cure the cause, your power release!

Finish the spell by thanking the Goddess for her assistance:
>*Goddess Hecate, I thank you for your aid.*

The spell is done, and the pain will begin to subside within a matter of minutes. You may need to repeat the spell each day until the pain is gone for good (to help establish a pattern of pain-relieving energies in the body).

HEIGHTENING INTUITION

The intention...

To heighten a specific person's mental and psychic intuition.

Physical preparations...

Make sure, before you begin, that you can touch, see, or hear anyone whom the spell is to affect. Alternatively, get a witness (such as hair, or a photograph) that can represent them. If your psychic abilities are very strong, you will be able to cast the spell by forming a psychic bond with them.

Clear your mind of unnecessary thoughts by repeating the words of the Divine Prayer to yourself (see page 1).

Magickal preparations...

Ideally, this spell should be cast on a Monday, due to the day's association with the moon and with intuition, divination, and psychic sensitivity. If the moon is in a waning cycle at the time of casting, concentrate on reducing random and unhelpful thoughts in the subject's mind. If the moon is in a waxing cycle, concentrate on building the subject's psychic link with their own Akasha (life force), which has access to information and images from the aethereal planes.

The enchantment...

Ask the recipients to lie down, close their eyes, and relax their body completely. Tell them that they must listen carefully to what you say as you cast the spell. Now place the palm of your left hand flat on the top of their head and softly utter the verse aloud:
>*In the cycle of the Moon,*
>*The seen becomes the unseen*

> And the unseen becomes the seen.
> By the power of the Moon,
> Your intuition may see what will be
> And what will be may be seen.
> All things may be observed by your mind,
> As your mind is part of all things.
> As the Moon does wax and wane in time
> So your perception with it may climb.
> Taking intuition from the high and the low,
> By Nature's order, it may be made so.

Now ask the recipients if they are willing to accept the spell into their mind:

> Do you accept this magick, which is of the ancient craft of Sorcery?

If they agree — and they should, unless they've changed their mind — then utter the verse in the positive context, as follows:

> In the cycle of the Moon,
> The seen becomes the unseen
> And the unseen becomes the seen.
> By the power of the Moon,
> Your intuition sees what will be
> And what will be can be seen.
> All things are observed by your mind,
> As your mind is part of all things.
> As the Moon does wax and wane in time
> So your perception with it will climb.
> Taking intuition from the high and the low,
> By Nature's order, make it so!

With the index finger of your right hand, draw the sign of the pentagram in the air in front of you to seal the spell, uttering:

> While the Moon waxes, so mote it be.
> While the Moon wanes, so mote it be.

The spell is complete.

Final actions...

Make sure that the recipients know that their heightened intuition will last only until the next new moon begins.

MANIFESTING AN IMAGE (ILLUSION)

The intention...
To cause an image to appear temporarily, or to alter the physical appearance
temporarily.

Physical preparations...
You need to have a very clear picture of the desired illusion in your mind
before you begin. The image in your mind is the image that will be projected
into the aethereal plane, which parallels the physical plane. You will use the
spell to empower the aethereal image, and use the four elements to create
the illusion in the physical plane. This spell uses psychic enhancement and
requires a very strong (well-trained) mind.

Relax, calm your mind, and get rid of all unnecessary thoughts and worries.
Make sure you're comfortable, and in a place where you won't be interrupted.

This spell is a little unusual in that you must first remove from your body
all metallic objects (jewelry, belt, and shoe buckles) and time-keeping
devices, including your watch, pocket computer, or electronic organizer. If
you carry anything metallic while casting this magick, that item might act as
a conductor for the energy you raise and either break or prevent the magick
from working (or both!).

Magickal preparations...
Ideally, this spell should be cast on a Friday, due to the day's association with
Venus, appearances, and all things visual. If the moon is in a waning cycle
at the time of casting, concentrate on reducing the physical appearance of
that which is real. If the moon is in a waxing cycle, concentrate on building
the physical appearance of the illusion.

The enchantment...
There is no verse to utter for this spell. It is all done with the power of your
imagination. First, you need to close your eyes and clear your head of all
thoughts, staring into the inner darkness of your spiritual mind.

Now picture the illusion that you want to project. Make sure you know
every detail, color, texture, shape, and line of the image. Next, you need to
carefully imagine the illusion appearing in a specific place in the real world
— forming the necessary bond between the aetheric and physical planes.

If you are "on location," open your eyes and envisage the illusion in place in the physical plane. If you are not at the location where the illusion is to appear, you need to know the location and be able to visualize it clearly in your mind.

Concentrate your psychic strength on merging the image of reality with the image of the illusion, and continue to do so until you can almost see the image yourself. It is at this point that you have created a strong aethereal illusion. Next, you need to draw and exhale three deep breaths for each of the four elements (fire, air, water, and earth), each time breathing in elemental energy from the cosmos and breathing out the energy into the shape of the illusion. With each breath you take, visualize the illusion taking shape in the physical plane until all four elements are present to their full capacity.

If you are able to see the illusion's physical location, look at it and you should now see the manifested illusion. (If you're not present, you just have to take it on faith that you have succeeded). If the illusion does not seem quite real to you or, as more often happens, it appears semi-transparent, you'll need to go back to the elemental breathing stage and try again.

Finally, cast the sign of the pentagram in the air (toward the illusion if possible) as a seal of the psychic magick and will-power that holds the illusion in place.

Final actions...

To break an illusion that you have cast, simply reverse the pentagram you cast earlier (by tracing the pentagram's five points in the air, but this time in reverse order) and command the illusion's energy to return to the cosmos. It is wise to close your eyes before you do that, because a broken illusion often emits a dazzling light briefly as it disperses.

FORMING AN AETHEREAL SHIELD

The intention...

To form an aethereal shield of protection around a specific person, object, or area.

This is a simple enchantment that protects a person, an object, or even a small area from unwanted aethereal influences.

Physical preparations...

As with most spells, your body needs to be in good physical health; otherwise, don't attempt this spell. And in order to clear your mind of unnecessary thoughts, try the positive visualization of calming scenes (the most popular are green fields, seashores, gentle rivers, and night skies). This kind of relaxation technique also has a balancing effect on your subtle energies. If that approach is not practical, repeat the words of the Divine Prayer (see page 1) to yourself until you feel relaxed, and ready to begin.

Magickal preparations...

Ideally, this spell should be cast on a Sunday, due to the day's association with the sun and with all things spiritual. If the moon is in a waning cycle at the time of casting, concentrate on decreasing spiritual threats or dangers. If the moon is in a waxing cycle, concentrate on building spiritual and aethereal protection around the person, object, or area in question.

The enchantment...

Hold your hands out in front of you with your palms facing in the direction of the person, object, or area to be shielded. If you are shielding yourself, place the palms of your hands flat against your chest with your arms crossed at the wrists to make a complete circuit for your body's energy (this is how the Egyptian pharaohs were posed when they were buried). Next, clear your mind and utter the following chant, or think it through in your mind:

> *Goddess pure and God divine,*
> *I beg protection at this time.*
> *Here until the New Moon is found,*
> *This* [person/object/place] *keep and now surround.*
> *Aethereal influence,*
> *Aether that harms;*
> *Keep* [them/it] *from danger*
> *And aethereal charms.*

Make the sign of the pentagram in the air with your right index finger and utter:

> *This shield of Aether I form from desire:*
> *New Moon, when it comes, will see it expire.*
> *Protection by Magick against harmful force*

Will keep the shield pure in Nature's true course.
While the Moon waxes, so mote it be.
While the Moon wanes, so mote it be.

The spell is complete.

Final actions...

The shield will last only as long as the current moon. If you have cast it for others, let them know this and, if possible, the date of the next new moon!

A final reminder: this shield doesn't protect from influences of elemental or other spiritual energies, nor is it a physical or emotional shield. It is purely a protection against aethereal influences. It forms an effective barrier to any aether-only magick that is cast at you.

If you need to dispel the shield before the next new moon, use the "Dispelling Unwanted Magick" arcane enchantment.

DISPELLING UNWANTED MAGICK

The intention...

To dispel the power of any unwanted magick that you suspect may be at work within a specific area, including magickally created illusions.

You can use this spell in a number of different ways, besides getting rid of a spell that somebody else has cast on you. You can dispel a magickal illusion, "uncharm" an amulet, talisman, or magick charm, and even stop one of your spells that's going wrong! But it's important that you don't work your magick carelessly, thinking you've got a kind of "undo" spell that can get you out of trouble. This spell won't reverse the damage your magick has done — it just stops it from doing any further damage!

Physical preparations...

Your mind needs to be clear and calm before you begin. Recite the Divine Prayer (see page 1) to yourself until you are ready to focus on the task at hand — the dispelling of magickal forces and energies.

Magickal preparations...

Ideally, this spell should be cast on a Saturday, due to the day's association with Saturn and with stoppage, limitation, and authority. If the moon is in a waning cycle at the time of casting, concentrate on the reduction of any magickal powers that are at work. If the moon is in a waxing cycle, concentrate on the breakage and disharmony of any magickal powers that are at work.

The enchantment...

Raise your hands in front of you with your palms facing in the general direction of the object, person, creature, or area that you suspect is under the influence of magick. Clear your mind of all thoughts and begin to concentrate on seeing the aethereal plane in your mind's eye, parallel to the physical plane in which we exist. As you begin to see the shapes and colors of the aether swirling and shifting, try to sense any unusual shapes that could be caused by unwanted magickal influences.

When you have isolated a possible magickal influence, concentrate on that area alone, slowly uttering (or thinking) the disenchantment:

Fire be extinguished, Water drained,
Air be thinned and Earth decayed.
Aether has come and Aether will go,
To dispel this magick. Make it so!

Continue to watch the aether patterns in the affected area. If there is any magick operating there, you will see the magick's pattern blur and fade as the aether and elemental energies dissipate and return to the cosmos, where they came from. If nothing happens at this stage, you may need to cast a magick circle and try again, this time invoking the Goddess and God and asking for their assistance. Some magick is too strong (or too well protected) to be dispelled in this way. This method is, however, sufficient for breaking the power of most illusions, curses, charms, and other enchantments.

When the unwanted magick has been broken, cast the sign of the pentagram in the air, using the index finger of your right hand, uttering:

As surely as I speak, the magick is broken.
I cast now this symbol as a true holy token.
Let not this mischief be reassembled.
So mote it be!

The magick has been dispelled, and you have cast a holy protection order in its place to prevent it from being recreated. Now ground (or rebalance) your body energies. A good meal is a sure way to ground yourself.

GLOSSARY

A

Active Magick. Magick that seeks to alter events or objects. *Also see* Divinatory Magick.

Aether. Spiritual (divine) energy, from which a living soul is made up. One of the five elements that work together in all of creation. *See* Elements *and* Aethereal Realm. *For the human spirit, also see* Individuality.

Aethereal Realm. The unseen realm of aether that holds together and defines the physical realm in which we live.

Air. One of the five elements that work together in all of creation. *See* Elements.

Alexandrian Wicca. A branch of the Wicca tradition of paganism, whose lineage derives from Alexander and Maxine Sanders.

Ambassador. Sometimes used to refer to a shaman (generally Western European).

Apprenticeship. The time spent in learning a craft.

Arcane Magick. Magick that operates outside of the commonly accepted laws of nature and physics.

Arthurian. That which relates to the ancient English legends of King Arthur. Also often used in reference to the Holy Grail mysteries.

Asperger (Aspergillis). Vessel used in ritual for sprinkling consecrated water or wine.

Athame. Commonly a black-handled knife used to cast magick circles, channel energy, etc. The handle is often carved with appropriate symbols along with the owner's name (usually in runes).

Attuned Harmonic Mind Magick. The process of sending a spell's essence to a subject telepathically (using only the power of the mind), short-cutting the need for a full spell-casting. Can be dangerous; use with caution.

B

Bell. Used in ritual to awaken or alert the elemental spirits. Not common practice ex-cept in some older traditions of witchcraft.

Black magick. Magic with evil intentions (which is against general pagan ethics). Also refers to ritual magic used to contact fallen angels (which does not fit with most pagan philosophy).

Blue moon. Referring to a single month in which two full moons are seen.

Bolline. White-handled knife used in ritual for cutting, carving, inscribing.

Book of Shadows (and Enchantments). The book of rituals, spells, and ethics that each magick user keeps. In many coven-based traditions (such as Wicca) the initiate copies this by hand.

C

Cauldron. A pot used in ritual for collecting ingredients or components of magick.

Celtic. A broad branch of pagan tradition encompassing Celtic Gaul, Western and Northern England, Ireland, Wales, Scotland, Brittany, and the Isle of Man.

Cernunnos. One of the names for the Horned God. Used in the Gardnerian tradition of Wicca.

Chalice. A cup or goblet used in ritual for holding or sharing wine.

Channeling. The process of directing aetheric energy from one place to another (also from one time to another). Can be dangerous if done without magickal protection; use with caution.

Charm. See Protective Amnulet.

Cleric. A term sometimes used to describe a religious or spiritual person, particularly in Sorcery or the Christian Church.

Cords. Narrow ropes used for the binding or releasing of magick. Also refers to cords or ropes of different colors worn around the waist to indicate levels of magickal or initiatory attainment.

Coven. Traditionally, a group of thirteen witches, but can be anywhere from three upwards who meet regularly.

Craft, the. A term frequently used to

describe witchcraft. Some pagan traditions use the term to describe their tradition as a whole.

Creation. Referring to the entirety of all that exists, seen and unseen. Sometimes used to refer to the physical realm as opposed to the aethereal realm. *Also see* Universe.

Crystals. Precious or semiprecious stones (also commonly quartz) that are able to collect or filter elemental energies.

Cymri. The main pagan tradition of Wales.

D

Divination. Using systems — such as the tarot and runes, or aids to clairvoyance such as crystal balls and black mirrors — to look into the future and discover hidden aspects of the present.

Divinatory Magick. Magick that seeks to observe or witness events, people, or objects without influencing them.

Dream-Weaver. A term sometimes used to describe one with telepathic or shamanic abilities, or one who is able to see accurately into the future.

Druidic. A collection of pagan traditions based on the magick and rituals of the Druids (the Celtic priests).

E

Earth. The planet on which we live. Also the name given to one of the five elements that work together in all of creation. *See* Elements.

Elementals. Conscious beings who inhabit the aetheric energy fields of the four elements: earth, air, fire, and water. Also entities created by magically breaking off part of the human aetheric energy field and imbuing it with a particular magickal intention or purpose.

Elements. Also known as "the Elements of the Wise." In magick the elements are earth, air, fire, and water, plus a fifth known as aether, akasha, ether, or spirit. They represent energy in different states.

Enactment. *See* Ritual.

F

Faery. *See* Tuatha de Danann.

Fire. One of the five elements that work together in all of creation. *See* Elements.

First Degree. The first level of initiatory commitment or attainment within a craft. Also see Witch, Priest, and Priestess.

Full moon The section of the Moon phases chart in which the moon is fully visible and illuminated (the opposite of a new moon).

G

Gardnerian Wicca. A branch of the Wicca tradition of paganism, whose lineage derives from Gerald Gardner (one of the first witches to publicize the Craft, and author of many early books on the Wiccan tradition).

God, the. The male aspect of the Creator, often seen as a strong, horned man. Commonly named Cernunnos (the Stag).

Goddess, the. The female aspect of the Creator, often seen as a beautiful young woman with flowing golden hair, dressed in rich red and blue robes. Other aspects of her character include the virgin and the hag, which reflect innocence and wisdom respectively.

Gods. Referring to the personification (or naming) of the aspects of the personality and attributes of the Creator. The ancient Greeks, Romans, Egyptians, Hebrews, and others named many different gods, but they all refer to some aspect of the one Creator.

Grimoire. Any book or collection of related documents. Commonly used to describe a book of spells and rituals. Also see Book of Shadows.

Grounding. The process of putting your body and spirit in contact with the earth in some way, to balance or replenish your body's energies. Harmony with nature is acheived by spending time in close contact with it.

H

Healer. Anything or anyone who has the inherent ability to heal the sick and cure particular ailments.

Heathen. Someone who does not acknowledge the God of Christianity, Judaism, or Islam. *Also see* Pagan.

Heaven. A term used by the Christian,

Judaic, and Islamic faiths to describe a place of eternal paradise to which they believe righteous souls go after their death. This is not consistent with pagan beliefs and runs contrary to the concept of reincarnation.

Hell. A term used by the Christian, Judaic, and Islamic faiths to describe a place of eternal torment to which they believe unrighteous souls go after their death. This is not consistent with pagan beliefs and runs contrary to the concept of reincarnation.

Heresy. An opinion or belief that is contrary to the teachings of an established religion (commonly used in reference to the Christian, Judaic, or Islamic faith).

Heretic. One who believes something that contradicts the teachings of an established religion (commonly used in reference to the Christian, Judaic, or Islamic faith).

High Magick. Magick that operates primarily in the aethereal realm without affecting the physical realm.

High Priest. In Wicca tradition, a High Priest may be any male witch who has received the second degree of initiation. Within any coven the chief male priest is normally referred to as the High Priest.

High Priestess. In Wicca tradition, any female witch who has already received the third degree of initiation may be considered a High Priestess.

Highest Initiation. Also known as the "third degree." The highest initiation that can be taken in any Craft, and not to be entered into lightly. It involves making a commitment to the God or the Goddess of the Craft.

I

Individuality. This is the eternal and divine part of us which endures after the body's death (and which, according to the theory of reincarnation, then incarnates in another body.) Some people call this "the soul," others "the self."

Initiation. A ritual designed to precipitate permanent changes in consciousness and spiritual growth. Outwardly, it is a recognition of commitment.

Inquisition. The name given to the councils of so-called holy men, who accused, tortured, and killed anyone suspected of being a witch during the time of the witch trials.

Invocation. A process by which the presence of the Goddess (or the God) is drawn into a magick circle, usually into the body of a priestess (or priest), and usually for help or inspiration. The word "invocation" (from the root word "invoke," from the Latin *invocare,* "to appeal to") can also refer to the summoning of a spirit by magickal means. Sometimes it can refer to the act of bringing a previously defined spiritual law, charm, or being into use.

J

Jungian. Psychological terms and theories devised by the Swiss-German psychologist, Carl Jung.

K

Karma Principle. See Law of Return.

L

Lamps of Art. Candles that illuminate the altar in ritual.

Law of Return. The principle that shows how your actions have equal reactions. Often summarized as "What ye plant, so shall ye reap." Also often called the Law of Cause and Effect, or the Karma Principle.

Laws of Nature. Referring to the unbending, self-governing rules by which everything in Creation operates.

Laws of Physics. Referring to the unbending, self-governing rules by which everything in the physical realm operates.

Left-Hand Path. Generally used to mean the practice of black magic. This is a misuse of what was originally a term from Indian tantric magic referring to the use of lunar/feminine energies (and which had no moral implications).

Low Magick. Magick that primarily affects the physical realm, utilizing the "As above, so below" principle.

Lunar month. The period of approximately 28 days in which the moon completes its full cycle.

M

Mage. *See* Magus.

Magick. The using or shaping of aethereal

energies to alter (or observe) people or events. *Also see* Divination.

Magickal Tools. Tools of a magick user, employed during ritual or spell-casting. Some tools may be enchanted for additional effectiveness.

Magick Circle. A circle of energy that a magick user creates in order to be protected temporarily from outside interference by beings or forces in the aethereal realm.

Magick Mirror. A darkened or blackened mirror used both in scrying and within the magick circle as a focus of energy. Also used as a portal to other aethereal realms.

Magick User. Anybody who uses magick, regardless of their Craft or tradition.

Magus (Mage, Magister). The secondary title usually given to second- and third-degree High Priests in traditions such as Wicca. It has been loosely used by lone practitioners and in other traditions to encourage respect or as a title of rank.

Meditation. The act of quietly contemplating, considering, or focusing on a subject or spiritual goal. Often used spiritually to achieve peace of mind and body.

Milesian. That which relates to humankind (as opposed to those of Faery- or spirit-kind).

N

Negative Polarity. Referring to a negative aspect (generally destructive) of a concept that also possesses a positive polarity.

New moon. The section of the moon phases chart in which the moon is not visible (the opposite of a full moon).

Norman Invasion. The invasion of Anglo-Saxon England by the Norman (French) armies.

O

Occult. (Literally "hidden.") A term used for magick and other esoteric arts and sciences.

Old Religion. A name often given to paganism (because of its roots in the ancient nature religions of the world).

P

Pagan. Generally speaking, a pagan is considered to be a person who is "outside the church" (of Judaism, Christianity, or Islam). *Also see* Heathen.

Paganism. The worship of a deity or deities predating Judaism, Christianity, and Islam. Sadly, it is quite common for paganism to be confused (by the uninformed) with black magic or even Satanism; any such ideas are erroneous.

Pantheon (Pantheism). (Literally "all gods.") The doctrine that the divine can manifest in many different forms and can be worshipped as a multitude of goddesses and gods. Pantheism is usually associated with the idea that "God is everything and everything is God."

Pen of Art. A pen that magick users keep specifically for writing in their Book of Shadows.

Pentacle. See Pentagram.

Pentagram. A five-pointed star shape that is used in magick to represent the perfect union and balance of all five magickal elements. It is also associated with purity and protection, and is sometimes used as a representation of the Goddess and the God in ritual.

Persona. (Literally "the mask.") The image of ourselves that we present to others.

Physical Realm. Referring to the physical world in which we live. *Also see* Aethereal Realm.

Plane. A plane or realm of existence, such as the physical realm or one of the many aetheric realms.

Polarity. A term used to imply the presence, or possibility, of two extremes within a concept (such as positive and negative, cold and hot, north and south, east and west, male and female, etc.).

Positive Polarity. Referring to a positive aspect (generally constructive) of a concept that also possesses a negative polarity.

Priest. The male equivalent of a priestess. Any male initiate of a spiritual or magickal tradition upon whom this title has been conferred. In traditions such as Wicca, this refers to any male initiate. In other traditions, the term may be used more sparingly. Lone practitioners might also adopt the title of priest as an outward sign of their progress or intent. *Also see* High Priest.

Priestess. A term often used to describe a female priest. *Also see* High Priestess *and* Witch.

Protected Place. Any place that is naturally protected from outside interference by beings or forces in the aethereal realm.

Protective Amulet. Any magickally empowered Talisman that serves to protect the user from outside interference by beings or forces in the aethereal realm.

Protective Enchantment. Any spell that serves to protect the subject from outside interference by beings or forces in the aethereal realm.

Psychic Enhancement. The act of improving or increasing the action of magick using the power of the mind.

Psychic Phenomena. Events relating to the manipulation or observation of events using only the power of the mind. *Also see* Telepathy *and* Telekinesis.

Q

Qabalah (Kabbalah). A Judaic magickal system widely used by Western occultists of various religious faiths. Many magickal concepts and ideals have been founded upon the Holy Qabalah (including Aleister Crowley's famous Thoth Tarot).

R

Rede. A code of ethics or moral guidelines.

Reincarnation. The belief that we are born, live, and die a number of times in order to gain life experience and achieve spiritual growth. Inherent in that is the idea that our individuality (our self or soul) continues after physical death.

Right-hand Path. Generally used to mean the practice of white magic. This is a misuse of what was originally a term from Indian tantric magic referring to the use of solar/masculine energies (as opposed to the left-hand path energies).

Ritual. A ceremony designed to produce certain spiritual and magickal effects. Ritual is commonly accepted as being a method of focusing attention on a specific task or desire in order to aid the mind in magickal workings.

Ropes. *See* Cords.

Rune. A spell or chant used for magickal purposes. Also an image of a carved character for use in writing magickal or private information. Also a divinatory system commonly using the letters of the Norse alphabet.

S

Salt bowl. An altar bowl that holds salt during ritual. It is often made of metal, with a pentagram engraved on the inside flat surface.

Samadhi. An expanded and enhanced state of consciousness achieved through contemplation and other spiritual practices, whereby the individual experiences a sense of oneness with the universe.

Satan. A figure from Christianity, Judaism, and Islam who personifies everything that is evil. This is not consistent with pagan beliefs or culture.

Scrying. A form of divination that uses a crystal ball, a black mirror, or a bowl of clouded water to aid clairvoyance.

Second Degree. An initiatory level of attainment within the Craft.

Shaman. Generally, a priest or priestess (often of a Druidic tradition) whose spiritual and daily life seeks to be in perfect harmony with Nature.

Sixth Sense. Refers to psychic ability (power of the mind) that works beyond the usual five human senses (sight, smell, taste, hearing, and touch). *Also see* Psychic Phenomena.

Skyclad. Ritual nudity.

Small Magick. Magick that works within the commonly accepted laws of nature and physics.

Solar. Referring to the sun, the central star of our solar system around which our planets orbit.

Solar Eclipse. Refers to when the daytime visibility of the sun is hindered or completely blocked by the moon.

Sorcerer's Code. The lengthy code of ethics with which sorcerers are advised to comply for the benefit of both themselves and others.

Sorcery. The Craft of magick that permits the use of Small magick and Arcane magick, natural and supernatural magick. *Also see* Witchcraft.

Spell. The aethereal intention created by words or thoughts to bring about some change by magickal means.

Staff. A tall wooden stick that can be used to store or discharge magickal energy at its owner's command.

Statues. Statues of the Goddess and the God are often placed on the altar during ritual.

Sword. Most commonly used in the casting of a Magick Circle, to mark out the boundary of the circle on the ground.

T

Talisman. Any jewelry or keepsake that has been imbued with some magickal intention or purpose. *Also see* Protective Amulet.

Telekinesis. The manipulation of physical objects using only the power of the mind. *Also see* Psychic Phenomena.

Telepathy. The ability to send and receive information between two minds using only psychic abilities (the power of the mind). *Also see* Psychic Phenomena.

Third Degree. The highest level of initiatory attainment within a Craft. *Also see* Highest Initiation.

Thurible. A small brazier for gently burning incense (for spiritual purification) during ritual.

Torah. The Jewish Books of Law (which also form the first five books of the Christian Bible's Old Testament: Genesis, Ex odus, Leviticus, Numbers, and Deuteronomy).

Tuatha de Danann. An Irish pagan tradition based on mythic tales of the Tuatha de Danann, the last Faery race before the Milesian invasion.

U

Universe. The full extent of creation as humankind currently knows it. Also sometimes called the Cosmos.

V

Vibrational Energies. Referring to all aetheric energy having a specific vibration or frequency at which it resonates. The frequency enables separate energy sources to work together or communicate on a subtle level.

W

Warlock. A term sometimes used to describe a male witch. Many witch traditions prefer not to use this term.

Water. One of the five elements that work together in all of creation. See Elements.

Water Bowl. An altar bowl that holds water during ritual, often made of metal, with a pentagram engraved on the inside flat surface. Sometimes a jug is used instead.

White Magick. A term used for magick with good intentions. Also used by some magicians to mean magic that contacts angels rather than demons.

Wicca. An Anglo-Saxon term for a witch or for witchcraft, meaning "wise one." Wicca is also the name of a popular (and possibly the most well-known) tradition of witchcraft.

Wiccan. One who is an initiate of the Wicca tradition of witchcraft. Some, however, prefer to say "I am a Wicca" rather than "I am a Wiccan."

Wiccan Rede. The eight-line witch code of ethics as dictated by the Wicca tradition. Sometimes abbreviated to simply "An ye harm none, do what ye will."

Wise man. A term sometimes used to refer to a male witch. Also used to mean a dream-weaver.

Wise woman. A term sometimes used to refer to a witch. Also used to mean a dream-weaver.

Witch. A practitioner of witchcraft. Some witches practice only magick, while others practice a spiritual path of witchcraft (such as Wicca).

Witchcraft. The Craft of magick that permits the use of magick in accordance with the commonly accepted laws of nature.

Witch Trials. An ugly period of religious fervor, dating from the 14th to the 17th centuries AD Those accused of witchcraft were tortured and killed for their alleged heresy against the Church. *See* Inquisition.

Wizard. A term often used to describe a sorcerer.

INDEX